THE MAGIC OF
THE WORD

May Rowland

Unity Books
Unity Village, MO 64065

Contents

Foreword 5

The Magic of the Word 7

Healing

    I Believe in Spiritual Healing 13

    Miracles of Healing 18

    You and Your Wonderful Body 23

    Stay Young, Alive, Alert 28

    Thanksgiving 33

You Are Needed

    You Are Needed 35

    Make Up Your Mind 39

    Your Soul's Highest Desire for You 42

    The Spirit of Happiness 45

    "None of These Things Moves Me" 53

    "Agree with Thine Adversary Quickly" ... 55

You and Your Abilities

    You and Your Abilities 61

    A Direct Approach to Right Answers 65

    Justice and Prosperity 69

    Prosperity Words 71

    Order 73

    Individual Responsibility 75

    The Divine Plan for Your Life 81

Thoughts about Special Times

    Your Most Fulfilling Gift 83

    An Easter Blessing 85

    Accept the Glory of Easter 87

Vacation Time 89
September Reminder 91

Worldwide Prayer
People Are Praying Around the World 93
Take Part in the Peace! 97

Questions and Answers
About Human Relations 99
About Practicing Truth 106
About Man as a Spiritual Being 113
About Death, Reincarnation 117
About Helping Others 123
About Healing 125
About Prayer 132

The Art of Meditation 145

Practice Feeling the Presence of God 149

Serenity through Prayer 155

Helps along the Way 161

Use the Working Power of the Holy Spirit 165

Finding the True God 171

When Storms Come 173

I Am the Christ within You 175

Affirmations from My Personal Notebook 177

Dedicated to
You!

Through Christ in you, you can live
life triumphantly and victoriously.

Foreword

In February, 1971, I gave up my desk (but not my ties) in Silent Unity.

At that time, as I thought about the word *retire* it brought to mind the buying of new tires for a car so that it can continue on its way. That's how I feel about it . . . I am re-*tiring*, and will be continuing on . . . not at my desk, but I will always be available when needed.

In the early days my father, Daniel Hoagland, became interested in Charles Fillmore's interpretation of the Bible. He joined Mr. Fillmore's first class of twelve members. Later my father became a Unity Sunday-school teacher and continued to teach for forty years. To help the Unity movement, my father mortgaged his property so that Unity could put up the buildings at 917 Tracy. He gave everything he had to it, because he had such faith in the ideas that Mr. Fillmore was presenting.

When I first commenced to work in Silent Unity, Charles Fillmore emphasized the idea that "Jesus Christ is the head of this work." Consequently I have never felt that Silent Unity was dependent upon any one special individual. It has always depended upon a group of workers dedicated to helping people through the wonderful Christ Spirit within them.

When I was appointed Director of Silent Unity, Myrtle Fillmore said to me, "You are a peacemaker." I have always remembered this, because she identified people with what they felt they were to contribute to Silent Unity.

In the years since the Fillmores started it, Silent Unity has continued to expand, grow, and reach more and more people around the world, because its chief cornerstone is Jesus Christ.

Wherever I am, I will always feel that I am a part of this great work. All of my life has been "in" the Unity work. I was born into it.

With the Silent Unity work in mind, Charles Fillmore wrote: "A company of persons gathered in the name of Jesus Christ can build a place in the ether and make it a continuous spiritual battery from which rays of energy and spiritual substance can be radiated to believing minds anywhere on earth. The Christ Mind will take up its abode in such a center of spiritual energy and cooperate with other minds in broadcasting health, wealth, and spiritual understanding everywhere."

Mr. Fillmore further stated: "Jesus Christ men are to be lights that glow and glow with a perpetual current from the omnipresent energy."

I believe that these ideas which Charles Fillmore saw so clearly are being fulfilled in the work of Silent Unity.

We are all fortunate to be a part of it.

These words from the Apostle Paul are very appropriate: "And my God will supply every need of yours according to his riches in glory in Christ Jesus. To our God and Father be glory for ever and ever. Amen."

May Rowland

The Magic of the Word

Remember, the power of the word is yours to wield. Through your word you change the circumstances of your life.

Use the magic of the word and remember that the word of God is quick and powerful and accomplishes that whereto it is sent.

A few years ago while on a lecture trip, I was asked by the sister-in-law of Cecil B. De Mille if I would care to go out to the studio. They were just finishing the shooting of the well-known picture "King of Kings," which portrayed, of course, the life and experiences of Jesus.

Mr. De Mille invited us to have lunch with him. His mind was still absorbed by the wonder and beauty of the picture, and it was as though he continued to live in the great story. The motion picture was a masterpiece, in which he had had a part. He had put all of his great genius and art into it and wanted it to be a true enactment of Bible times. All who saw it recognized its greatness, and experienced the feeling that they were living with the great Bible characters.

I was seated next to Mr. De Mille at the lunch table in the studio. He fairly vibrated with the great truths he had put into picture form for the world to see.

He turned to me abruptly and asked, "Do you know what it says in the first chapter of John?"

It happened that I knew the chapter very well, as do

many Bible students, and I quoted the words:

"In the beginning was the Word, and the Word was with God, and the Word was God. He was in the beginning with God; all things were made through him, and without him was not anything made that was made. In him was life, and the life was the light of men. The light shines in the darkness, and the darkness has not overcome it."

Mr. De Mille then asked, "Do you know what the Word means?"

Before I could give my opinion, he said, with great enthusiasm: "*Logos* was the word used in the original Greek and represents the creative power of the Mind in every man."

In order to be exact in producing "King of Kings" Mr. De Mille and his associates studied the Scriptures very carefully, as well as what some of the early Greek philosophers had to say about the Logos, or Word.

When John said, "Without him [the Word] was not anything made that was made," he was stating a great truth. One of the secrets which has not been revealed to most men is that the word we use every day is the symbol of the creative power of God. Our words, out of omnipresent substance, form the ideas we bring into expression.

The word moves through a world of energy and vibration, and substance takes form as we decree. We are learning more and more about the world in which we live. We are coming to realize that it is a world of energy, atomic power, a world of vibration. In Hebrews, chapter 11, verse 3, it states that the world was created by the "word of God."

Many of us overlook the power that is ours to use. The words we speak have power. They mold our life; they are the formative expressions of our thinking. Words bring our dreams into expression; they enrich and expand our life. There is miracle-working power in the word.

We have heard the expression: Your thinking can change your world. But our thoughts are expressed in words.

Perhaps it has never occurred to us that our own individual world is created by the words we speak. We set certain vibrations into motion by the use of words. Not realizing this, we find many things in our experience which we do not like, but we are not aware that we have had anything to do with what we experience.

A few years ago the laser beam was discovered, a ray in which light is not diffused but goes directly to where it is sent. Scientists predict great things for it.

When I think of the Word of God, I think of it as similar to the laser ray—it goes directly to where it is sent. The Bible says: "The word of God is living and active." And

"So shall my word be that goes forth from my
        mouth;
    it shall not return to me empty,
  but it shall accomplish that which I purpose,
    and prosper in the thing for which I sent it."

We are putting the word, the working power of God, into action every day.

The real word is the word that the Christ speaks through us to heal, to bless, and to transform lives. Christ, the living Word, spoke through Jesus to restore those in need of healing.

The living Word is like a word of command. It speaks through man when he has become aware of the Christ within himself.

All through the New Testament we have the positive expression of the word of truth, put into expression by Jesus. Jesus realized and accepted His responsibility as the voice of God. He spoke living words which we can use today. He told us to keep His sayings.

Everyone who reads any of the Unity literature knows about our affirmative prayers. *Daily Word* gives us one to use every day of the week, throughout the month.

Affirmations state principles to live by that we put into action in our daily life. Thousands of persons are helped each month by these affirmations of Truth. Some people call them prayers; some call them affirmations. They are really affirmative prayers and suited to the needs of people everywhere. These affirmations become literally our "daily word."

Through using affirmative prayers, our mind is trained to think positively and to think about the truth of our being. In reality each one of us is essentially a spiritual being, filled with limitless power, well equipped to live a full and rich life.

The vital word that illumines, heals, and prospers can be spoken through us to bless the needs of the people we meet, either in our home, in our business, or in the world about us.

Prayer is the lifeblood of the Unity work. It is the backbone of all our undertakings. Unity people become masters of prayer because they practice it constantly. We organize our life and our work on a foundation of prayer.

Jeremiah, the prophet, said, "Let the prophet who has a dream tell the dream, but let him who has my word speak my word faithfully."

This is what we are asking you to do, not only to have a dream but to bring the dream into fulfillment through the words you speak.

People frequently ask us what they can do to bring about peace in the world. We tell them that they can do something about peace in the world by commencing to radiate it to their own individual world, starting within themselves and in their own households.

With love in our heart let us proclaim to our individual world: "Let the peace of God rule in my mind, in my heart, and in my world. Let my heart, my home, and my individual world always be peaceful and harmonious." This is one way we can start using the power of the word to bring good into our life and to let it flow from us into the world.

To any tumultuous thoughts around us let us say, "Peace! Be still!" To any negative thinking within ourself we can say, "The joy of the Lord uplifts and blesses me all day long."

Hosea said to the Israelites:

> "Take with you words
> and return to the Lord."

Should you feel depressed remember these words: *I will look unto the hills from whence cometh my help.*

To discouraging thoughts:
I thank You, God, that all depressing, discouraging

11

thoughts are melting away, and I am at peace.

Should you feel lonely:

"Lo, I am with you always." I will satisfy your longing soul.

Should you need healing:

Through Christ in me I am made whole, praise God.

Should you need help to regulate and prosper your affairs:

The Spirit of God within me is the source of my supply. He directs me in what I am to do, and adjusts and harmonizes all my affairs. I am abundantly prospered.

It is also very effective to write down your affirmative prayers. This helps to establish in your consciousness exactly what you want. After you speak your word, then if you wish, write it out and put it in an envelope or some place where you can forget the problem for the moment and let your word work.

Remember, the power of the word is yours to wield. Through your word you change the circumstances of your life.

Use the magic of the word and remember that the word of God is quick and powerful and accomplishes that whereto it is sent.

Expect miracles to happen in your life, and they will! And do not forget to say, "Thank You, God."

Healing

I believe in spiritual healing. I believe that we are essentially spiritual beings. I believe that we can have a body full of light, shining with health.

I Believe in Spiritual Healing

In this age of change we are becoming more receptive to new ideas, we are becoming more flexible in our thinking. The old stubborn states of mind are giving way, and we are learning many new things about life. Surely the time is long overdue for us to get some different ideas about ourself.

I believe in spiritual healing. I believe that we are essentially spiritual beings. I believe that we come alive with health, vigor, and vitality as we accept these very important words of Jesus: "When your eye is sound, your whole body is full of light; if then your whole body is full of light, having no part dark, it will be wholly bright."

I believe that we can have a body full of light, shining with health.

I would like to give you a new concept about yourself so that you will never again think of yourself as old, sick, weak, tired, or incapable. Age does not make us old, nor bring ill-health. What does so are fixed states of mind, especially those that bow us down with negative

13

thoughts and feelings.

Man is so closely woven in spirit, soul, and body that the thoughts he keeps in mind find quick expression through his soul and body.

There is a need to get cooperation between the mind and the body. Healing is a matter of cooperation with the forces within you.

The body should be recognized as equal in the trinity—spirit, soul, and body.

When the body refuses to do its work properly man gets very much perplexed with it and resorts to all kinds of remedies that do not get at the cause of the difficulty, and relief is only temporary.

If you say you are sick, weak, or old, it is the very nature of your body to cooperate with what you say, because you are the authority in your own body temple.

If you want to have a beautiful, healthy, strong body, then you must cooperate with it by approving of it, by giving it life-giving, health-giving ideas.

Charles Roth, one of our Unity ministers, suggests that we use ideas like the following:

"I am relaxed. I am peaceful. There is only one presence and one power, God, the good, omnipotent, and this presence and power is expressing itself through me now.

"I bless my body.

"I thank my body. (How wonderful it is for us to appreciate what the body constantly does for us! This idea is a real blessing to your body.)

"I thank my subconscious mind for its untiring supervision of my bodily processes.

14

"I lean back into the everlasting arms, and rest in God's love.

"I praise God from whom all blessings flow."

In healing there is a very important point that most persons overlook. Perhaps they say or speak healing words over and over but do not seem to have the reward of good health. I believe the reason for this is that the individual has failed to listen to what he has been saying or praying about.

For instance, if you say, "God in the midst of me is mighty to heal," then you need to know that everything in you is listening to these words, accepting them, and meeting in agreement with them, no matter what the appearances may be at the moment. Through meeting in agreement in your conscious mind with these ideas, your subconscious mind picks them up and puts them into expression. So the oftener you say living words—and listen to what you say—the quicker will you attain results in your bodily healing.

Start with a simple idea. Tell the forces of your being that the intelligence of God is directing them to bring peace, harmony, and wholeness into every part of your organism.

You will commence to feel a flow of health. Who is doing the healing? God is. But you are directing the light and energy within you to do its perfect healing work. You are recognizing His forces moving in and through you.

Charles Fillmore in his writings says that we hold the body in mind as an idea. What kind of idea do you have of the body?

Man's body is not a mechanical instrument, set to go

15

till it runs down. Man's body is an expression of the Spirit of God within him. In the highest sense it is the temple of the living God.

The body may be physical, but it is not material. It is made up of waves and forces and vibrations. Every atom in the body, of which there are trillions and trillions, has at its center what some scientists speak of as an atomic center, or a center of light.

The body is not dense, heavy, or material. It is light, substance, and intelligence, and responds to the ideas you have about it. In fact, it is so cooperative that it listens to everything you say about it.

Can you commence to realize what a brilliant center of light your whole body is? Science proves what Jesus taught. He was speaking literal truth when He said, "I am the light of the world."

Try thinking of your body as a great center of light. Think of it as constantly being charged and recharged with vibrations of light, giving forth energy. Think of your body as not only giving forth energy but producing harmony in a musical and rhythmical pattern. Some of our scientists are bringing to our attention the fact that the body is like a great musical instrument, that its keynote is music, not matter.

Since our keynote is music and not matter, we commence to see that the answer to our need for healing is harmony in our thoughts and feelings.

We start our healing work by taking an idea of harmony and order into our mind, and then by thinking of the body in a loving and understanding way, we learn to relax into a feeling of peace and harmony. We can use a word of prayer that brings the idea of peace, order, and harmony, for instance, "God in the midst of me directs all my organs and functions into a harmonious pattern."

Mentally agree with the idea you use. Even though temporarily you do not feel that what you have said is true, just keep using the idea. Try mentally to agree with it until your subconscious mind takes it up and its truth becomes established. You want to be well. You want your body to feel peaceful and harmonious. Then work with the idea you want to feel expressing itself in your body.

Know that God's energy, life, and intelligence are moving in and through every part of your body, doing a perfect healing work in you. Tell yourself that never again will you think of yourself as sick, weak, old, tired, or incapable, that you are through with the old ways of thinking about your body. Think of yourself as a spiritual being, think of yourself as alive with health, vigor, and vitality, filled with light and shining with health.

Miracles of Healing

God is an instant, constant source of help in every need.

We have seen this truth proved literally thousands of times in the Silent Unity work.

I have seen the power of Truth at work practically all of my life. I have discovered that a little faith, when used, will bring about miracles.

Early in my experience in Silent Unity, I witnessed a miracle. A woman who had a grocery store near the Unity offices called me in Silent Unity one morning and said: "I am bringing a baby over to you to heal. She is dying!" I do not know that this woman had great faith, but she called on Unity as a last resort. You can imagine the urgency of the moment and my feeling of inadequacy. But knowing that this was an emergency which I must meet, I prayed for faith and courage and I went to see this woman and the baby.

I've always remembered what Jesus said about faith as a grain of mustard seed, and at that moment this was about the size of mine. However something within me said, "Do not fear, I am with you." I looked at the baby in the carriage and summoned up my faith to know that God is the healing power and that this child was in His hands.

Soon the baby made a move in the carriage and the woman, who was the child's aunt, was satisfied and wheeled her home.

This was my first experience in seeing a miracle of

healing take place. Undoubtedly the aunt's faith was at that moment greater than mine.

Twenty years after this experience a young woman called to see me at my office in Silent Unity. She came to tell me that she was the baby the aunt had brought to me. She wanted me to see what a healthy, happy individual she was. Part of the miracle of this healing was for the girl to come back so many years later to remind me of that healing and to thank Silent Unity for it.

Since then I have witnessed healings all through my life. To witness a so-called miracle is to stand aside and let God work through you. In other words, in any healing work we cultivate the practice of God's presence until it literally takes over. God uses us to express His power and authority to heal.

In any healing work, we turn ourself over to God so that His power can pour through us, so that His perfect work can be done through us.

Should you see someone in need, remember that God is your instant, constant source of help in every need. Think of God as the great, omnipresent good which only needs recognition in your consciousness. As you feel His all-enfolding presence within, around, and about you, His miracle-working power is released through you, and you are a channel through which He does His mighty works.

God's love and power are always ready to express themselves through you at any time, and especially in a time of need.

When you see circumstances and conditions that need help, let God's power through you pour out a blessing upon the situation. It is surprising how the

19

most dire circumstances can quickly turn for the better when a blessing is given.

Silent Unity is a great healing center and no one person in Silent Unity takes any individual credit for the work. We realize that we are consecrated and dedicated to do God's work and that He uses us as a group for His channel of healing.

We always feel that you wonderful ones who are praying with us are very important to the Silent Unity work. You are strengthening the work through your prayerful cooperation.

A few years ago while on a tour around the world, a woman who was part of our tour group read *Daily Word* and also had great faith in the Silent Unity work. When anyone in the group did not feel well, she would tell them to see me, and she would assure them that prayer would help them.

In Turkey, a woman who was part of another group had become ill and it looked as though she would not be able to continue with her tour. The friend who was so interested in Unity met me at the elevator with this woman by the hand. The woman commenced to tell me how the doctor had told her that she had caught some kind of germ from the food and that it might be a very serious kind, that she might never get over it.

When people are on the move like this, there is no time for long explanations. I talked with her a few moments and told her to think about God as her health. I assured her that there was nothing to fear, and I told her to think about this line from *The Prayer of Faith*, "God is my health, I can't be sick." She had been in bed for several days, and this was the first time she had come down to the lobby.

The next day as we were leaving for Jerusalem, there she was, waiting for me, with someone else by the hand, wanting this person to meet someone from Silent Unity. She herself was feeling fine.

We know that the word of Truth is quick and powerful. Christ, the living Word, quickens and heals.

Another time on this same world tour, a woman fell on the polished floor of her room in Bangkok. She could not move and was taken to the hospital. The outlook was very dire. It was reported that she might never walk again, and that it would be weeks before she could be moved or flown back to the States.

Her sister came to me as she did not want to leave this woman in that faraway country and was planning to stay with her. She was crying and frightened by the hopeless look of the situation. Right away I said: "We will not accept this report. Through the power of God she can be healed."

I gave her a prayer to take to the hospital to her sister, and also asked her to use it.

The next day the report was better, and by the following day this woman had made such remarkable progress that she could be taken in a wheelchair to the plane, and the doctors now said that she would be all right. She went with us to India and the other places around the world with no difficulty.

Through these experiences I discovered that one does not necessarily need to have understanding to be healed. One needs only to have an open mind. When people are greatly distressed, they are receptive to help wherever and however it comes. *one must have the belief*

In these situations I couldn't in a few moments expound the principles that Unity teaches. I just had time to speak a positive word of Truth. But it brought results. I had believed that with God all things are possible, right now, but these experiences strengthened my belief.

God is an instant, constant source of help in every need. You can prove this truth in your life and you can be a channel through which God blesses others.

You and Your Wonderful Body

Do you ever stop to thank God for your wonderful body? God created you to express His life and love, and eventually to show forth His perfection, even as Jesus Christ was God's perfect expression.

Gratitude is a loving expression of thoughtfulness on your part. For even small kindnesses we should express appreciation. If you appreciate a loved one in your home, do not be timid about saying, "I love you and I appreciate you." To express a feeling of thankfulness goes a long way with all of us. It breaks down barriers; it expands a loving attitude in us.

There is no friend closer to you than your body, and it constantly follows your directions. As you express appreciation for the life of God moving in and through you, freely and rhythmically, the body responds with harmony and health.

It is good to remind yourself often that God is the source of the life within you and that you are His expression. Make the most of this wonderful gift of life and cultivate the joy of living. If you can catch the feeling, even for a moment, that all is right with you and your world, the feeling will come back to you time and time again. It is the Spirit of God within you welling up to express the joy within you.

God's life flows into every atom and function of your body and does not overlook any part. Your feeling of gratitude for this gift of life can be felt from the top of your head to the soles of your feet, and it is a real blessing to your whole organism. Praise God that you are fully and joyously alive!

Just as plants and flowers respond to loving attention, so does your intelligent body. It loves to be appreciated and to be blessed with strong words of encouragement. You can thank your hands, your feet, your heart, and all of your organs and functions, every member of your body, and praise them for their cooperation in all that they do for you.

Have you ever realized that the very life you feel at this moment is the life of God within you? There is no other source of life or any other kind of life, no matter what kind of an idea you have held about it.

Sometimes people have an entirely wrong thought about the body, and they think of themselves as old, ugly, unwanted, and unloved. What do you think this attitude of mind does to your body? Beauty starts with the thoughts you think about yourself and about life in general. If life to you is humdrum and you find no joy in living, it is time to change your attitude. You can do this by praising and giving thanks to God for His free-flowing life within you. You can base your thinking on an entirely new premise about life, and you will be transformed by the renewing of your mind.

The life of God within you is beautiful, always beautiful, and no matter what you think about your body, it is still the temple of the living God.

God is the source of life within you. Think of this life as a renewing, rebuilding, revitalizing quality moving in and through you.

Jesus understood and appreciated the life, intelligence, and light within man. His great purpose was to

24

awaken man to his own divinity. When we are told to
follow Jesus and to keep His sayings, we are inclined to
think this just means to be good or to be sanctimonious
in a negative kind of way. To follow the teachings of
Jesus is to accept the challenge of a very active, vital
way of life. It includes the idea that our body is the
temple of the living God. We must recognize and believe that the body is an important part of the trinity,
spirit, soul, and body.

In our Unity way we always think in terms of putting
good ideas into expression, and we do this by making
affirmative prayers out of our helpful ideas. We put the
substance of the idea into concrete form so that we can
remember it and refer to it and use it. This is a way of
growth. It is not just a matter of reading something and
laying it aside. Rather, we take the good idea into our
consciousness and think about it, meditate upon it, so
that it will take hold in our mind.

Your body is eager to be told the truth, so commence to bless it with living words of truth. For instance, the following affirmations are good ones to use
and to make a part of your consciousness:

"Life is continuous and eternal."

"The life I feel, that I am aware of at this very
moment, is God-life, eternal life. It revitalizes and heals
me now."

Let me remind you of one of Charles Fillmore's early
prayers about life. We can use these words as an affirmative prayer:

"The glorious infusion of the more abundant life of
Jesus Christ vitalizes me, and I am lifted up and
healed."

Think of the tremendous hold Jesus had on life, which was sufficient to resurrect Him. Then realize that you have access to this same resurrecting life, the very life of God within you. Surely now is the time to be renewing your mind with life-giving ideas. Teach yourself to think of what you call "my life" as God's life moving in and through you. This will give you an entirely new approach to life. Then every time you think of life, you will associate the life which you call "my life" with the eternal life of God.

Even your brain cells can be recharged through thoughts of praise and thanksgiving. Say to yourself:

"I praise and give thanks that the Christ life flowing in and through my brain cells quickens and rejuvenates my mind."

"I am thankful that my mind is keen, alert, and inspired with wonderful, free-flowing ideas."

"I am thankful that I have a good memory, revealing to me quickly what I need to know."

"I am thankful that my body is radiant with youth, vitality, and beauty."

God created each one of us out of the substance, life, and intelligence of His immortal being. Think how great you are and start a flow of appreciation to the source of your being. You will begin to feel how beautifully and wonderfully you were brought into being.

Even if you momentarily feel "down and out," let go false ideas about yourself and think about your spiritually originated being. Commence to feel the glory of the Lord within you. Praise and give thanks to God for His unlimited life flowing in and through you.

The apostle Paul gave us great ideas about the body.

He said, "Do you not know that your body is a temple of the Holy Spirit within you, which you have from God? . . . So glorify God in your body."

We glorify God by letting the radiance of His presence shine through us.

God did not create us and leave us to work out our own salvation. He put His Spirit within us, which we call the Christ. This Christ is within every man. When we say that the body is the temple of the living God, the idea itself implies that we turn within to worship and to praise and to give thanks to God. When we become quiet enough, we can feel the harmony, order, and peace that await us.

As we quietly listen to the words, "Be still, and know that I am God," we become aware that God is our source. Then as we praise and give thanks to this all-enfolding, radiant presence within, we are truly glorifying God in our midst.

"Be still, and know that I am peace."

"Be still, and know that I am life."

"Be still, and know that I am love."

"Be still, and know that I am the everlasting One."

Stay Young, Alive, Alert

I like this subject because I like to tell you how wonderful you are and how wonderful God created you to be.

You are very important to God because He created you to be His perfect expression.

The next time you feel run down and at the end of your rope, try giving thanks to God as the source of your life and energy. You will feel a refreshing stream of life renewing your mind and body. God created you a living soul and continues to breathe into you the breath of life.

Jesus came to show us the true character of life. Remember, He said, "I came that they may have life and have it abundantly." He did not indicate that He was preparing us for a future life, but for our present abundant living. We sometimes think that the truths Jesus talked about were just for His immediate followers, that they have nothing to do with us. But Jesus taught eternal truths. The mission of Jesus Christ is to show us that man is an eternal being.

Renewal and healing come through a constant recognition of this truth of the divinity within you. There are spiritual energies within you that rebuild your body and maintain it in vitality and youthfulness. When you realize this, you become enthusiastic about living. Nothing can limit the life and renewing power within you when you commence to glorify God in your body.

Life is a gift of God to each one of us. It is absolutely

unlimited, except in our concept of it. We sometimes say that life is consciousness. Our consciousness is made up of what we constantly think, feel, and believe. We express life on the level of our consciousness. This becomes the overall picture of our life's expression. What we sow into our consciousness every day about life brings either a feeling of joyous life or a feeling that we are getting old and that life is passing us by.

When we recognize the importance of taking positive ideas into our consciousness, often words come to us that are important to our progress. One time these words came to me: "I am young, strong, beautiful. My body knows it, and my body shows it." This simple thought has helped to strengthen my feeling of eternal life and youth.

Our body is a willing and loving cooperator with our thoughts and words. When we think about ideas of life and meet in agreement with them, the ideas are taken up by the subconscious and put into expression through us.

Life does not grow old. It constantly renews itself. As we become conscious of the truth that God is the origin and the source of the life within us, we develop a different feeling about what we call our life. We realize that this life which has its origin in God is everlasting, eternal.

The time limitation is one of the mistaken ideas that has restricted us in our life's expression. This is a man made limitation. Man is only half awake. He lives within his own limits. But God has not placed any limits on him. God created man not for time but for eternity. God created man as a living expression of His own abundant, eternal life. Therefore, let us identify ourselves with God's abundant, ever-renewing life, rather than with the idea of time and limitation.

Adelaide Reynolds was an actress who did not start her career until she was seventy. She passed away a few years ago at the age of one hundred. When she was forty-three, she was told that she was too old to hold a job. This was her reaction: "I went home and tore the birth and death notices out of my Bible. I wasn't going to be the sniveling slave of time. Who counts how many times the earth swings around the sun!"

Adelaide Reynold's simple formula for success: hard work, prayer, and gratitude, and remembering that there are no obstacles in life—only challenges.

Since it is not important how many years we have lived, let's stop counting them. And let's not embarrass people by asking them their age. Let's forget the idea of growing old and commence really to live.

A man of forty who was attending night school was asked why at this age he was back in school. He answered, "Because I do not want to die at forty and wait to be buried at eighty." Many persons in adult education classes are learning new professions—studying medicine, law, architecture.

Right now is the time to get a clear concept about life and to commence to sow seeds of life into our body consciousness. Charles Fillmore says that we carry the body in the mind as an idea. So let's carry the idea of a perfect body in our mind.

Sometimes people say, "I'm too old to take up these new ideas." Our consciousness about renewing life starts first in our thinking and we are never too old to think. We might just as well cultivate a positive and joyous attitude and really enjoy life.

What are some of the limitations you have placed upon yourself that keep you from expressing the joy of living? Have you ever said, "Well, at my age I can't expect much from life"? Do you watch life from the sidelines instead of entering in and enjoying yourself? Do you live in the past and talk only about the good old days?

Change these habits. Enter into a joy-filled present. If you wish to be young and buoyant, do not carry a lot of burdens in your mind. Sometimes a person will think he cannot carry a bag of groceries from the car into the house, but he carries an impossible load of burdens in his mind. Limit the load on your mind.

Robert Updegraff said: "Youth is a matter of attitude, not of calendar years. It flows from inner springs concealed in most of us. If only we can manage to tap it, it is a spring which waters and freshens the imagination and the spirit." Mr. Updegraff also says that one may go through old age and come out on the other side, that it is like going through a tunnel. He says it can happen to anyone between nineteen and ninety, and that it is never too late to venture.

Jesus came with a message of life and joy. In Unity we are trying to prepare people to live and enjoy life. If you would stay young and vital:

Let old thoughts and old conditions be as waters that have passed away.

Find new interests.

Arouse within yourself a love of life.

Try new things.

Let the idea of yourself as a spiritual being become the dominating idea in your mind. When it is, your life will no longer be affected by the limitations that bind the natural man.

As you learn to pray with an idea of the spiritual nature in mind, you will release powers, energies, and forces that will heal and renew mind and body. Think of yourself as perpetually young, robust, buoyant, vigorous. Think of every atom of your body as alight and alive with the life of Christ. Life is continuous and eternal. The life you feel at this moment is the eternal life of God, flowing in and through you to renew you completely.

Thanksgiving

Have you ever thought of God as the health of your body? Have you ever stopped to think that in Him you live, move, and have your being? Have you ever realized that it is God-life which is now expressing itself in your body?

There is no life apart from God and no health apart from God.

We have tried to think we could find health apart from God, but the search leads round and round and eventually back to the ever-flowing fount of God-life and health within us.

Most of us have found God a present help in time of stress. When we have called His name in time of trouble, we have found His presence uplifting and satisfying. Our burdens have dropped away. The same power which can adjust our affairs and take away our burdens can renew and restore our body.

Jesus understood this and He called upon the all-loving Father to heal and to restore, even to resurrect into newness of life. He turned to the Father in a spirit of thanksgiving. We too have learned to turn to the all-loving Father in a spirit of thanksgiving.

When we open our heart to God in a spirit of gratitude and thankfulness, His love descends upon us in overflowing measure. God has given Himself to His children. He does not withhold His good at some times and give abundantly at other times. He is giving His life and substance through us constantly. But we must open our heart and mind and acknowledge His presence. Through this thankful attitude we receive.

We may not be experiencing physical inharmony. It may be that we are trying to conquer inharmony of another sort. Perhaps we have not learned to control our temper; we may be irritable and cross. We may need more courage and strength to meet our problems. Perhaps we lack poise and patience. No matter what the need may be, the all-loving Father hears the call and will answer. There is nothing to fear; there is nothing to fight. The all-sustaining love and life of God are always here, always present, always with us.

"Father, we thank Thee that Thou art the source of our unfailing health. We thank Thee that Thou art with Thy children everywhere. We rejoice in Thy love and life which are unfailing, unchanging, eternal. Father, we thank Thee that Thy life and love flow constantly in and through us, protecting, sustaining, strengthening, and renewing us."

34

You Are Needed

Find your happiness and satisfaction from within your own being and do not look to someone else to give it to you. Do everything you possibly can to make others happy, but also develop your own inner peace and satisfaction.

In every generation the cry of young people has been: "Let me stand on my own! Let me live my own life!" This reaching out for new ways, new ideas, new ideals makes for the development of the race. It is difficult for parents sometimes to realize that their children do not love them less because they feel the need to try their own wings.

The mother bird is patient in teaching the young to fly, but when they are ready to leave the nest, she releases them. She has taught them all she can. We can release our children in the same way, knowing that we have taught them "how to fly."

If parents try to carry all the responsibility for the children, they can never develop into mature human beings. It is inspiring to see how self-sufficient young people can be. My admiration is great for the young people of today who are learning to handle their own affairs and live their own lives. Some young people, of course, are not mature enough to act wisely. They may for a time follow courses of action that seem confused or misdirected; but the parents who have done all they can to help their children during their growing-up time to have a sound sense of values, need to stand by in trust and faith and know that these children have within them the guiding light of God's Spirit to help them find their way.

The person who is too possessive in his love always has a difficult time of it. This is especially true in the case of parents who do not want to let their children be on their own or act on their own. Parents who do not try to possess their children, find themselves closer to their children, even when the children are away and living lives of their own.

I knew of a woman who cried for days when her only son decided after college not to return to the small town in which he grew up. The mother was heartbroken, not because her son had failed her—he was a fine promising young man—but because her dream of always having him nearby had been shattered.

This is the point I want to make: just as young people need to live their own lives, to grow and to develop, to reach out in their thoughts and aspirations, so do all of us.

I talk with many persons who feel lonely and neglected because their children are grown and they no longer feel needed or wanted. There are some persons who let themselves wither away because they find themselves at a loss to know what to do with their lives. For so many years their lives have centered around the demands and needs of a growing family.

If we feel this way, we should ask God to open up new ways to us of finding happiness, joy, freedom, satisfaction. "God's love is deep within me, ever satisfying my soul." Build your life anew upon this idea. No matter what your family status, this is a good idea for your own development. Find your happiness and satisfaction from within your own being and do not look to someone else to give it to you. Do everything you possibly can to make others happy, but also develop your own inner peace and satisfaction.

Many of us have a longing for something and we do not know the reason for the dissatisfaction we feel. Something within us is reaching out for fulfillment. We may have a soul desire that the conscious mind does not comprehend. No individual or outside thing can satisfy this longing. Inner peace and happiness come through knowing that God satisfies our longing souls and fills our lives with His good.

A friend who took hold of this idea, "God satisfies my longing soul and fills my life with His good," says that it opened her eyes about herself. She hadn't realized before that all through the years she had carried the attitude of "stay on your side of the fence, and I'll stay on mine." Nor did she realize that (in her own words) "my pet desires were just plain human will." She says that she knows now that God has ways to satisfy her soul—and in so many *unexpected* ways. This realization has given her a sense of freedom and a greater joy in living than she ever experienced before.

We are never too old to learn new things. I remember hearing about a man who was living in a retirement home. Though way up in years he was studying Spanish. His friends could not understand this. But he enjoyed trying to learn a new language and liked keeping his mind active. All of us should find some special interest and take every opportunity to develop unused, and sometimes unsuspected talents. Grandma Moses started painting when in her seventies and became one of our well-known artists. She painted from memory scenes of her childhood. She is just one of the many wonderful individuals who have found life joyous and satisfying because they refused to give up or to feel old or unwanted.

When you know that God loves you with an everlasting love and that His love is deep within you, ever satisfying your soul, you will be filled with a sense of completeness; you will know and feel that your life has meaning and purpose.

Make Up Your Mind

In order to meet life joyously and successfully, we all need to cultivate a positive attitude toward life. This will give us a feeling of being in tune with the good and will help us bring it forth. After all, it is our attitude toward life that brings us joy in living.

To cultivate a positive attitude toward life, we should put our faith in some strong and positive idea. Instead of letting circumstances and conditions rule us and make us unhappy and resistant toward things that happen, let us accept an idea like this: "God is the ruling and sustaining power in my life. I place everything that concerns me into His care and keeping." This idea holds true, no matter what we have to face. It does not free us from having to meet circumstances and conditions, but it arouses our faith in the principle of good and in the knowledge that God is in charge. It gives us a positive outlook, which is always followed by a right solution to our problems.

It is up to each of us individually to decide how we will react and how we will handle situations that confront us. If we are negative in our approach, a problem is apt to hang on. What happens in our experience is not as important as how we react.

The first step necessary to help us stand firm is to make up our mind not to be disturbed and distressed over things going on around us. When we learn to control our emotions we become centers of peace, poise, and strength.

The power of God within us is on the job, ready to uplift and bless us the moment we are calm enough to give it a chance. Through this recognition we find a tremendous power at work that brings peace, order, and harmony into expression in our life.

When we see things in the lives of other persons which seem distressing or unfair, instead of sympathizing with their problems, thus magnifying them, let us make up our mind that we are going to be of some real help to the individual needing it. We are going to know that good is coming out of the disturbing situation, no matter what the appearance is. We are going to know that God is in charge and we are going to stand by our principle of good.

There may be times when this is not easy to do. It takes mental control to be able to stand firm when things do not seem to work out as we would like them to. If we have been resistant or fearful, let us say to ourself, "None of these things move me." Let us know deep down within ourself that God, the good omnipotent, is in charge and that all things will work out in divine order for us and for all.

It helps us in developing a positive attitude if we make up our mind not to be resistant or disturbed when someone says something which is unkind or unfair.

Problems in the home can be handled easily and quickly if we make up our mind right now, that we will be loving, understanding, and kind to the members of our family and to all whom we meet. If we keep our own peace and poise and loving attitude, we will be a real blessing to our own family and our loving attitude will radiate far beyond our immediate family to bless

40

all the people whom we meet.

We can train ourself to be a center of peace and harmony in our home, our office, among friends or strangers. Instead of finding things to criticize and find fault with, we can learn to be a harmonizer.

Through Christ in us we can be strong, dependable, reliable. Our emotions will follow our thoughts, and our life will be harmonized and blessed.

Your Soul's Highest Desire for You

Many of our needs for healing come from the very depths of our soul. We think of the soul as including the subconscious phase of mind, which stores all the memories of the past. Often we find ourself filled with feelings that come out of our past experience, feelings which have not been satisfied or redeemed.

For instance, if we have made mistakes and have not handled our feelings of guilt, these buried feelings may be the cause of restlessness or depression. The desire of the soul is for our feelings of guilt to be healed, but we may not know just how to go about it.

Our habitual thinking reaches to the depths of our being and either disturbs the calm peace of our soul or enriches our life with strong ideas about our spiritual nature.

Georgiana Tree West has made the statement, "You are where you are and what you are because of your habitual thinking."

Commence to think of yourself as a child of God. Believe in His strength to protect you, to sustain you, and to bless you daily.

Say to yourself, "I accept the forgiveness of Jesus Christ for all my past mistakes, and they are entirely wiped out." As you do this you have a new sense of freedom and uplift. The heavy weight is gone.

Another good prayer to use is, "I am in tune with the highest desire of my soul." By accepting this idea of being in tune with that which is highest and best, your most sincere, heartfelt desires commence to take shape.

After you have used some specified strong and positive ideas to help yourself, you will find your own ideas expanding. You will know how to direct your life into constructive channels.

As you commence to do this, you not only will discipline your thinking but will also feel yourself stronger in your spiritual nature. You are then on your way to overcoming and to bringing into fulfillment your soul's highest desires.

No matter how much wealth one may have, no matter how harmonious his home life is, he still needs to feel happy and satisfied within his own soul. The plan for man on earth is to develop his spiritual nature, from which all the happiness, satisfaction, and joy he desires will come into expression.

We are only restless and dissatisfied with life because we have not yet realized and expressed the power of our spiritual nature.

Emerson tells us where we need to start: "Nothing can bring you peace but yourself. Nothing can bring you peace but the triumph of principles."

These principles are the good ideas upon which we must base our life.

Hundreds of persons write us or tell us about their overcomings through following the practical helps given by Unity. The Unity way of prayer is not complicated nor hard to understand. But we need to pray daily to arouse the spiritual nature within us, from which comes power and authority in our life to control our moods, to control our thinking so that our soul is at peace, so that we are in tune with and bring into expression the good we are seeking.

We may not always consciously be able to know what the highest desire of our soul is, but the knowledge is within us; and if we put ourself in tune with the spiritual forces of our being, we will find ourself growing and unfolding in ways that are wonderful.

As we tune in to our soul's highest desire for us, we will find an entirely new sense of freedom—freedom to express the greatness within us—and we will no longer worry about what our future holds. The way before us will be made clear for us.

The Spirit of Happiness

"Bless the Lord, O my soul;
   And all that is within me, bless his holy name!"

Have you ever been so filled with joy that this Scripture sprang from your heart to your lips, and you thrilled with the ecstasy of living? If you have not yet touched the wellspring of joy within you, then sing this paean of praise to yourself until the deep waters of your soul have been stirred and their healing started to every part of your being.

The power of a blessing of this nature is so great that it not only brings healing to the body but reaches out and transforms your environment.

Sunlight always dispels darkness. The radiation of light from a prayer of praise and blessing casts out the darkness of error. Joy, thanksgiving, and praise bring light into our world, while sadness, depression, and gloom cast long shadows on our paths.

Because some of us do not know why these shadows cross our paths, let us uncover the errors back of the shadows, with the idea in mind that we are overcoming them and casting them out of our life. The limitations of the personal man are really not worth mentioning, except that by uncovering them we are better able to free ourself from them.

Have you ever thought that most of the unhappiness in your world comes through selfishness? You are unwilling to give up the petty things. You want some individual to do just as you think he should do; or someone has done something that you do not like and that you are unwilling to forgive; you cannot see why someone treats you as you have been treated and why everything that you do goes wrong. Perhaps you are harboring thoughts of self-pity and injustice until you are a veritable cloud of depression. The remedy is to stop thinking so much about yourself; stop thinking that everything that happens will affect you personally. By thinking of self you are keeping your good away from you. Your sunny neighbor, who forgets self and is kept busy letting his light shine, is attracting more and more of the good that you so much desire. He has learned the joy of giving and serving, and because he has fulfilled one phase of the law the reaction brings back to him innumerable blessings.

Then we find the sorrowing one who says of the happy individual: "Oh, yes, it is easy for him; he has never known sorrow, while my whole life has been filled with it. Life is just one great disappointment." This unhappy individual does not realize that he is hugging his sorrow and grief. Perhaps the happy, radiant person has gone through the purifying fire of self-denial and learned his lessons before becoming the inspiration that he is. Those people who are happy are happy because they have stood the tests that came to them. They have learned to rise above conditions and to master self. They are real overcomers.

True happiness is unconditional, not dependent upon persons or things. It is not the hilarious expression which comes to one when something especially pleases, and the next moment is turned into unhappiness when something goes wrong. True happiness is that firm, strong, unwavering substance of joy which cannot be touched by the variation of mortal thought. The one who has touched this spirit of joy feels the strength of it constantly sustaining him; no matter what may seem to go wrong in an external way, you will find him master.

Do you think he could have gained this mastery had he never overcome? No, mastery does not come so easily. He has risen above conditions all along the way, and is not only serene, poised, and happy when all is going well in his life and affairs, but he can stand unmoved during the storm; he meets the test, and overcomes. In the face of impending evil he finds that he is still at peace with God, and he rejoices. He it is who has built a strong foundation which cannot be moved by wind or floods. "Every one then who hears these words of mine and does them will be like a wise man who built his house upon the rock; and the rain fell, and the floods came, and the winds blew and beat upon that house, but it did not fall, because it was founded on the rock."

Our faith should be placed in God, the good omnipotent. When one is anxious and worried he is unhappy, but when he places his trust in God he is lifted above worry and anxiety; he abides in peace. The Christ light shines through him in all its gentle radiance, and not only purifies his own life but radiates to all those whom he meets. It comforts those who come near him and brings peace to the hearts of those who seem burdened with care.

One of the many things that will bind us to limitations and shut out real happiness is personal will. We should make it a part of our daily practice to let go of personal desire, that the Christ may more fully express in and through us. Say, "Not my will, but thine, be done." When we say this, and mean it, the Christ spirit takes possession and attracts to the individual even greater good than he could anticipate for himself. The personal man's vision is limited; consequently man calls forth, through his personal will, conditions that are not always desirable.

Most of us become involved in the working out of plans that we feel we could not possibly give up. Good judgment may show us that the steps considered are not wise, but personal love, being selfish, wants to cling. We may repeat the words, "Not my will, Lord, but thine, be done," before we reach the state of consciousness in which we really mean them. Our cherished ideas are held so closely to us that they seem to be a part of us. Finally, though, when it dawns upon us that heretofore we have merely said the words, we are willing to give up everything held in a personal way: personal attachments, personal ambition—everything. When this stage in our spiritual evolution is reached, we are overwhelmed with the desire to "let go," and the human will is merged with the divine will. In a very short time all that has seemed so involved works out in perfect order, and we reach a state of poise and happiness previously unknown. Courage and strength are

48

required in the giving up of a cherished idea into which we have put much substance and thought, but with each renunciation a little more of the personal consciousness is transformed. After a while we can say, "The will of God is my will, for I am His perfect expression."

When we know the truth we shall have no need to go through such a process of denial, for we shall follow the better way all along the path of life.

One who desires to be happy does not place himself in bondage to personal attachments. He learns to loose his relatives and friends. He loves them with a broader, more universal love, and contributes to their happiness instead of bothering them with petty thoughts that they have mistreated him, that they have slighted and misunderstood him.

Free yourself every day by placing your dear one in the care and keeping of God; say, "I am not bound by personal limitations; I am free with the freedom of Spirit." This affirmation will help you come over into the path of light where little personal things become unimportant, and you will begin to appreciate life in a more comprehensive way. Cultivate a feeling of fellowship with all people, instead of limiting yourself to the little circle in which you have been living.

Climb the mountain path that leads to the heights; lose sight of the miniature world in which you have been living. Learn to look upon those things that are enduring and eternal, and be free from personal bondage.

Gossip is an enemy to happiness. When we understand that the human is so close to the divine in each of us that sometimes just a little encouragement will help another individual to find the real in himself, we shall try to make our heart the abode of love, and shall look with the spirit of love upon every man. When our heart is filled with love we will not criticize or condemn those with whom we are associated. We will make it our business to become pure in heart and to see all other souls in the same light of purity. We shall be able to discern that which is good and true and desirable, but we shall leave all judgment to the Father.

God's love is so broad that when it has full expression through man it is not cognizant of evil. It sees all things in their original perfection. It does not deal in trivialities—it recognizes the good, the true, the perfect.

Just as the wisdom of God works through man as pure intelligence, just so love works through man as pure feeling which recognizes itself as the love of God in every individual.

One who feels the mighty power of God's love surging through his being need never say, "I am sick," for the love of God heals; nor, "I am poor," for the love of God attracts all good; nor, "I am unhappy," for the love of God satisfies the longing soul and fills the yearning life with good.

Let this be the antidote for every irritable, cross, critical thought: "Divine love, manifest thyself in me."

Divine love seems to encircle our world as an atmosphere of golden light. One enters into divine love by letting the thought of love express itself through him toward all; through meeting every condition in a loving attitude.

Where you are concerned, let nothing but love manifest itself. Let it express itself through you until it radiates through the cells of your body; then you really will be letting your light shine.

Touching many souls in various ways, you will bless them all. One who comes to you in great sorrow will find compassion, the compassion that one overcomer feels for another. Perhaps you have the memory of just such an experience as he is passing through, and you, feeling the joy of the overcomer, can speak words of courage and strength to help him into the path of light.

Man has sought satisfaction in ways innumerable through the world's so-called pleasures, but he has found, as did the prodigal son, that he must return to the Father's house, that he must seek God within his own soul in order to find happiness. Then, no matter what his hands may momentarily find to do, he does it joyously, because he is working for the Lord.

All the restlessness, dissatisfaction, and inharmony expressing in you are calls in the soul of you to come up higher—to look Godward. The people with whom you live, or those with whom you are associated cannot be the cause of your inharmony. Search yourself, and you will find what is wrong in your world. Don't shift the responsibility. Only through mastery is joy attained. Assert your dominion over your thoughts, and it will not be long until you find that you are gaining the mastery over circumstances. Do not be discouraged if the overcoming is not made all at once. "Count it all joy, my brethren, when you meet various trials, for you know that the testing of your faith produces steadfastness. And let steadfastness have its full effect, that you may be perfect and complete, lacking in nothing."

51

The panacea for all inharmony is God. Find Him and recognize your unity with Him. Then the very spirit of joy will enter into you and you will know that the king of glory has come in.

"None of These Things
Moves Me"

Everyone has enough to do to keep control of his own feelings without becoming depressed by the upsets of other individuals.

If someone comes to you with a problem, more than likely he wants your support to overcome the problem. He has come to you for help, not for you to sink with him into the depths of despair.

When an individual takes on the problems of another individual and becomes emotionally upset about these problems, he can be of little help to the one in need.

There is a right answer to every situation, and as you ask for guidance and inspiration in helping those who come to you, whether neighbors, friends, business associates, or relatives, seek divine guidance and give help from this level.

Some persons are apt to dramatize their problems, because it gives them "center of the stage" attention. If you enter into the situation and feel sorry for such persons and agree with them as to how difficult everything is, you can be of no help. Two of you are in the problem, then—two of you sink into despair. You have put yourself on the level of the problem, and one of you needs to come up higher.

Remember Paul said, when surrounded by difficulties, "None of these things move me," meaning that he refused to fall into negation or despair about anything.

By taking your stand and not allowing yourself to

get disturbed and worked up over the personal affairs of others, you are able to be of real help.

In Truth we learn not to identify ourselves with the dissatisfactions of others. Involvement does not mean weeping for the world but becoming involved in knowing that God is in charge, that God is love, and that with God there is a way for things to be made right.

"Agree with Thine Adversary Quickly"

When we are in need of guidance and direction in our lives, many times words from the teachings of Jesus come to mind. These words prompt us, through the still, small voice within, and inspire us to right action.

One time when I hesitated to face a challenge in my life, these words came to me: "Agree with thine adversary quickly, whiles thou art in the way with him." The rest of the text in the 5th chapter of Matthew (A.S.V.) implies that, if one does not agree quickly, there may be a more complex situation to handle. I acted on this idea, and there was no longer any "adversary." The Revised Standard Version of the Bible uses the word *accuser* instead of *adversary*. This translation reads, "Make friends quickly with your accuser." Most adversaries, or accusers, are in our own mind. They are our negative thoughts or feelings that we need to do something about.

If you are facing a situation which you dread, pray for guidance about it, knowing that it has come to you to handle quickly while "thou art with him in the way." You can turn any adverse circumstance into a real blessing when you face it with courage and confidence in God's power within you.

For instance, if someone is unkind to you, rebukes you, or belittles you, you may carry an unhappy, unforgiving feeling in your mind for a long time until it becomes an obsession with you. Even if someone has

55

criticized you unjustly, let it go! Free your mind!

How can you free your mind? In your present state of mind you may not be able to see beyond the unhappy circumstance or condition, but you can allow yourself to be liberated from this condition, or state of mind, if you are willing. Recognize that the Christ within you is the liberator!

I believe that love and forgiveness are the answer for anyone who has a problem to solve, no matter how large or how small it is.

Sometimes we wear ourself out going over and over the mistakes we have made in the past, and feeling sorry that we didn't act differently toward someone. We should recall that "whenever our hearts condemn us, . . . God is greater than our hearts, and he knows everything." The mistakes of the past come to the surface of our mind so that we can free ourself from our own self-made bondage to them. We need to accept the forgiving love of Jesus Christ, knowing that this forgiveness reaches to the very depths of our being and into every part of our nature—mind, soul, and body. Through this method we will reach freedom, and the old ideas of the past will be forgotten and will not return to bother us any more.

all bondage is self made

An affirmation that helps us to be forever free from thinking about and reliving the mistakes of the past is: *"The forgiving love of Jesus Christ reaches to the depths of my being and sets me free from mistakes of the past and the results of mistakes of the past."* We can free our mind through using these ideas.

Old ideas that have been stored up in the subconscious mind can be cleansed and purified and redeemed through this acknowledgment of power in the name of Jesus Christ.

"You will forget your misery;
    You will remember it as waters that have passed
        away
And your life will be brighter than the noonday."

We need to put love into our forgiveness of our own past mistakes and also into our forgiveness of others we may have held in bondage. We want our forgiveness to be more than just words. We make forgiveness powerful and effective as we put our hearts into the idea.

An adversary we need to be freed from is the belief that our happiness is dependent upon the actions of other persons. Each of us is responsible for his own happiness. I have heard many people say, "If he (or she) would just change his (or her) ways, we would get along fine!" Resistant and critical thoughts about others become opposing forces in our mind.

We might as well face this fact: We cannot afford to be unforgiving or unloving. Love and forgiveness are the basic harmonizers that this great world of ours is most in need of. These qualities are necessary in our development if we are to enjoy life and to be free.

It is good to give a silent blessing to anyone who appears to be thoughtless, unkind, or unfriendly, and to let love radiate from our heart, to forgive and bless. When we do this, the power of divine love takes hold in us and in the other individual as a great constructive, harmonizing power. We feel the unifying action of love taking over in the situation, and we are able to release it.

None of us can afford to be unkind, critical, or condemnatory in our attitudes. Wrong thinking and wrong feeling go hand in hand.

Many scientists and physicians are recognizing the ill effect of our mental attitudes on our bodies. An interesting article in the Kansas City Star was entitled "Sow a Remark and Reap a Disease." The idea was brought out in a conference of physicians at the Menorah Medical Center, as a new concept. Unity has taught for years that wrong thinking has a very definite effect upon the body. The article referred to this idea as the "engram concept," which states that feelings and words leave an impress on our brain cells, changing them biochemically and storing up a memory that becomes part of our health and personality. The article stated that "engram is the concept's name for a cellular impression, a trace, a physical change, a memory, left in nature's wonder computer, the brain, which directs the body's physical processes and also links them to the outside environmental world." This idea of the interrelation of mind and body is gaining credibility among more and more physicians, according to Dr. Philip Bergman, a professor of clinical neurology at Mount Sinai School of Medicine, New York.

A friend told me recently that she finally had a complete healing of a fractured leg. She said that it took four months, but that it was her own fault that the healing was slow, for in her subconscious mind she was holding resentment toward the woman who was to blame for the accident. Even the doctor said that my friend must forgive and forget. Otherwise, it would take longer for the splintered bone to heal. The friend said that through this experience of trying to forgive she became closer to God than she has ever been.

Daily in all that we think and say, we are making impresses, not just on people around us, but on ourselves. This is why the practice of daily prayer and the reading of something positive and constructive every day forms good impresses, healthy impresses upon our very brain cells.

We can learn to be positive, constructive, and dynamic in our thinking and speaking so that we continually bless our mind and body. This is another way to "agree with thine adversary quickly." As we let the radiant, overcoming Christ Mind in us direct us, we shall be free, happy, and at peace with ourself and with others.

You and Your Abilities

The world is full of people, young and old, who are finding new ways to enjoy the good things in life through relying on their inner resources to guide them. Whether they realize it or not, they are relying on the all-knowing Mind of God within them.

Innate within every man is the ability to take care of himself. This ability needs to be aroused and used by all of us.

Every man is in reality in business with himself, as surely as though he owns a business where he sells commodities. Some of us are good businessmen and some of us are not. Some of us do not realize that we are in business. We think we are working for some firm, and that perhaps we do not get much out of the job. Usually we think that we do not get all that we deserve. I am sure that many of us do not feel that we are ever paid enough, no matter what we receive from the position.

When one realizes that he is in business with himself he commences to look over his stock, to see what he can do to prosper and progress and to increase his business. He soon discovers whether or not he is using all of his salable material and whether or not he is a responsible individual.

When he takes inventory he finds all kinds of things he can do to make himself a prosperous businessman.

In the beginning of the Unity work the Fillmores laid the foundation for its success upon good, sound spiritual principles. One of these principles was the law of giving and receiving. They went first to God for ideas, and then commenced to use these ideas in their own lives, to the very best of their understanding and faith.

It wasn't too long until there were others who wanted to help in this ministry. Where was the money coming from to recompense these individuals? They were told that they must have the faith to fulfill the law of giving and receiving. They must have faith in their efforts to help others and faith in the law to bring them compensation. They had to give first of themselves in loving service, with understanding and faith in God and trust that there would be sufficient income to take care of their living expenses.

It is the individual's business to bring forth his ability, his strength, his wisdom, and the undeveloped possibilities within himself to give the world something worthwhile—something it is willing to pay for.

The tangibles in one's mind are not enough to guarantee his success. He needs to direct his ability in some active way, not just hold it in his mind. He needs to get to work in some practical way. So many people, who are brimful of ability, go through life not making any practical application of their abilities. They do not concentrate or make the effort to do anything about the abilities or ideas they have within them. A businessman has to have his stock in shape to sell. Many of us fall short here. We do not have our abilities in shape to sell. We do this and we do that, and perhaps we pray, but this is followed by a lack of direction of our effort. I would say to these people: Ask God to direct your talents and make them salable.

What are you doing to get rid of your old stock of limitations? Old stock of any kind will not sell. Get rid of your thoughts of old age, inability, laziness, and your lack of willingness to put forth some effort to concentrate on an honest-to-goodness, straightforward effort toward success. Don't be afraid to work. It will be your salvation. Let go all thought of what you can't do.

I know a man who was educated in Europe and spent many years in India. When he came to this country he could not at first get into the field to which he was best fitted, and he was capable along many lines. He had good health and strength and a willingness to work. He had always been responsive and responsible to God and to himself, trying to improve his abilities and conscientiously working to make his talents bring forth results.

This man, past middle age, in a new country where he did not have a foothold, volunteered to do anything, and he meant *anything,* because he knew within himself that if he could put the simple abilities he had to work, even on a bargain counter, he could later sell his greater ability. He wrestled baggage, drove a station wagon, and no job was menial to him. Needless to say it was not long before the way opened for his right employment, where he could use his ability and training.

Many times we grudgingly do little about our small abilities, thinking they are beneath us or not worthwhile, or do not pay enough, and we give no effort toward putting them on the market. They are not important to us. We are looking for "big deals" and important things to do. We are not as wise as the businessman who sells the small items and thereby prospers. Everyone has some salable qualities and abilities. Think yours over and put them on the market. Do not just say, "I am willing to do anything," and then turn your back on all the things there are to do. Give value in your dishwashing, in your office job, in your restaurant, in your sweeping of floors, in handling baggage, in driving a station wagon. If you are able to put these abilities on the market you can also sell your greater talents, and what is more, *you* will be discovered in the effort you are making.

A Direct Approach
to Right Answers

In meeting the everyday affairs of life, we are always searching for right answers. Nearly every one of us has unexpected circumstances to meet, and our first thought is: What shall I do about this? What is the right answer?

If we can train our mind to be open and receptive to the Mind of God within us, and turn to this Mind instantly when there is something to meet, we will receive direct and inspiring ideas. We will know what to do and how to do it.

Through this all-knowing Mind within you, you can learn to think clearly, to comprehend the situations before you, and to be guided in the right action to take. Through the all-knowing Mind of God, which has been within you since the beginning of time, you are enabled to think clearly and understand easily. You know what you are to do or say, what steps you need to take.

Never let your mind get in a rut or into a groove. Know that your mind is open, receptive, flexible. You can meet circumstances and conditions with open mind and heart, and with courage.

I remember one time when I had to take a special examination and had to learn some new things along the line of the examination. I used the idea that the all-knowing Mind of God was with me to see me through every experience, no matter how difficult. I recognized that through this all-knowing Mind I was able to think clearly, comprehend the subject, and re-member whatever I had to learn. Needless to say, I passed the examination perfectly.

The Mind of God within you makes you alert so that you can understand new or unexpected things quickly. Keep your mind always alert; never let it get sluggish.

As you turn to the all-knowing Mind of God within you, you will be freed from anxiety about the outcome of any situation: whatever you have to do, you will understand what is required of you. You will be able to follow through easily, and with perfect timing.

The Mind of God within you is always on the job. Train yourself to rely on this great source of inspiration within you. It is always willing to show you the way, to give you right direction.

Let your mind be open and free and joyous as you remember your unity with the great Source of knowl-edge within you.

Times change, you change, circumstances and condi-tions change. You can constantly expand and grow and unfold if you will keep yourself open and receptive to new and inspiring ideas.

You have heard someone say, "Well, my mind is made up, and I won't change it." This individual be-comes set and rigid and critical. One who is not willing to change his mind seems to have a hard time in life. If he is of the older generation, he may become critical of younger people.

Many young people call on us to help them pass their examinations in high school and college. Let me say here that I think the young people all across the coun-try who are growing and unfolding and who are sure to be a blessing to our nation and to humanity are in the majority. It is good to acknowledge this, because of the many negative reports we hear about the youth of our time.

One summer recently while traveling in Europe we met many young people, most of them college students, and they had the admiration of the adults because they were self-assured. They had confidence in their inner resources to guide, direct, and protect them.

When we were standing in line to have our passports checked as we were going from Malaga, Spain, across to Tangiers, in front of me was a young man whom almost anyone would classify as a hippie. I've always gotten along well with young people, and I thought of this as an opportunity to see how this young man was thinking. He had shoulder-length hair, a shirt that looked as if it had been washed in a creek (and it probably had been); he carried a pack on his back, indicating that he was sleeping wherever he found a place. I asked him where he was going. He said, "Well, I'm going down into Africa and roam around here and there." As I inquired about his experiences he was very willing to answer my questions. I asked where he had come from. His home was in California, and he had been called into the service. He had served his time in Vietnam and had saved up some money. He intended to travel over the world until it was used up. Then he would go back to the States and to his home in California. We had an interesting conversation and I found him to be a very intelligent young man. I admired his spirit and courage in using the money he had saved to travel around the world. This would be an education in itself, and not an easy one, sleeping for the most part out-of-doors and carrying his belongings on his back.

The world is full of people, young and old, who are finding new ways to enjoy the good things in life through relying on their inner resources to guide them. Whether they realize it or not, they are relying on the all-knowing Mind of God within them.

I like this Bible text: "I have filled him with the Spirit of God, with ability and intelligence, with knowledge, and all craftsmanship."

Think of yourself as filled with the Spirit of God: in all that confronts you, take the stand that you have the all-knowing Mind of God within you. This gives you a direct approach to right answers, no matter what the need or situation.

Justice and Prosperity

What a sense of peace and freedom comes to one when he turns over the responsibility for his affairs to the Lord!

Sometimes a person will struggle along for years, claiming something he thinks belongs to him which he feels is unjustly withheld. He may think that others overwork him and misuse him, that someone has the power to take away from him something that belongs to him. Seldom does he stop to think that there is a law of order and balance at work in this world of ours which adjusts and governs everything, and that if he but learns to cooperate with it, he can never be unjustly treated.

We all need to learn that no one has the power to withhold that which rightfully belongs to us. The law of divine justice is as accurate as the law expressed in these words: "Whatever a man sows, that he will also reap."

If in your place of business you have the feeling that your employer or those with whom you work are not just and fair with you, balance your worth on the other side and see if you have measured up. A small fraction of weight throws the balance to one side or the other.

We all want to do what is right, and it is because our human standard is not always accurate that we get out of balance. When we proclaim that the justice of the Lord is at work in us, we bring a mighty power into action which will adjust, harmonize, and correct. There is nothing that cannot be straightened out through the law of divine adjustment. Set it to work in your affairs through proclaiming, "My justice comes from the Lord, and I trust Him to regulate and to prosper all my affairs."

Prosperity Words

No matter how much a person may have in an outer way, he still desires more until he gets hold of the soul-satisfying idea that develops prosperity. It is not riches alone that man really wants, but the power to develop riches. That was the power Jesus attained. As a result He brought forth all the outer things needed.

One may become prosperous by building up a large thought about money, but he will not have the satisfaction that goes with a true prosperity consciousness. He thinks that if he has money he can buy whatever else he needs to make him happy. This is not true. Furthermore, it is the long, hard road and does not lead to contentment.

Let us, as students of a higher law, understand where to begin. All life's rewards—health, happiness, and prosperity—come about through the development of our own individual consciousness. So let us start at home.

Think about the following affirmation: "Life and substance, love's unity, embrace, enfold, and prosper me." The mere repetition of such words will not make anyone prosperous, but if you think about words that have a vital truth back of them you will open your consciousness to ideas that will prosper you.

Life. Substance. Love.   These are three very important and essential words in the development of a prosperity consciousness. We are all conscious of some measure of life, but most of us are automatons in its expression. We think we have life because we have inherited it; we do not think much more about it. We should recognize God as the source of our life and feel His energizing, vibrating power in every cell of our body. We should always be alive, alert, and awake.

Be joyous, be happy, be enthusiastic about the good things of life. Stir up the latent life and energy within you by talking and thinking about life. Bless your work by putting into it a new spirit of life. See it astir with renewed activity. Don't let your world go to sleep. You, through Christ, are at the head of things. You are the master. Don't limit your capacity by your personal feeling about things. God works in and through you in an unlimited way when you give Him a chance.

Now think about the word *substance*. Substance is the underlying principle out of which all things are formed. If our words have enough life back of them they will mold and form substance and bring the desired good into visibility. Eventually we will attain the same consciousness Jesus had when He called forth the loaves and fishes and fed the multitude.

Added to the idea of life and substance there must be love. Love is the great attracting power. It binds and holds together that which is good and pure and repels that which is unlike itself.

"Life and substance, love's unity, embrace, enfold, and prosper me." With these ideas to start with, you can build a prosperity consciousness which is enduring, and the good things will be added.

Order

"Order is heaven's first law." There is no question about this, for we all recognize the fact that there is a law of order which governs the universe. One cannot conceive of the confusion there would be upon the face of the earth were the universe devoid of order.

Just as order governs the universe, so should it manifest itself in the affairs of man. If one's thoughts and actions are not orderly, one's affairs will show confusion.

One of the causes of confusion in our affairs is procrastination. We sometimes put off from day to day the things which should be handled at once. We let things pile up, and disorder results.

When a new idea comes to one, after due consideration, he should act upon it. If the idea has possibilities, there is no reason why it cannot be put into operation. It is the ideas that come and are put back into the mind without being acted upon that cause disorder in the mind and later in the affairs. If a person finds, after thinking it over, that the idea which has come to him would not be of any special benefit if put into operation, he should put it out of his mind entirely. It should not be allowed to become part of a confusion of ideas that bob up ever so often demanding attention.

After acting upon the ideas that have possibilities, then one's house should be put in order. If the clothes closets and all the extra space in one's house are filled with accumulated stuff, he should begin to pass these things along. Let order be established! It is surprising how free a person feels when he has cleared out these congested spaces.

An orderly person is efficient in all that he does. If he is in an office, his desk is kept in order. He is prompt in keeping appointments. Promptness and order go hand in hand and tend to make one successful in business affairs.

I once knew a woman who was continually wanting to know what was wrong in her affairs. Everything she touched seemed to go wrong. One need not have known her long to observe that the one thing most needed was order. For instance, in her room things were so piled up that it was difficult to enter it. Her general appearance was disorderly. She moved from one place to another to get away from her own disorder. In making one of these moves, part of her belongings fell out of the moving van. Still she asked, "Why?" The last I knew of her, she was hunting for a position where all would be quiet and harmonious. It is needless to say that a position of this kind could not be found in her state of mind.

The persons who know true freedom are those who are orderly in their thinking and acting. True freedom is freedom that is earned, and it does not interfere with an orderly system or the freedom of another person.

As Paul says, "All things should be done decently and in order."

Individual Responsibility

One of the chief cornerstones in character building is responsibility. This characteristic spells the difference between failure and success in business, and is also one of the foundation stones upon which a happy home must be built. In all the affairs of our daily life someone must be held accountable; most of us feel that it should be the other person.

We are sometimes accused of being a nation in which few people do original thinking. We would rather let someone else take the responsibility and do our thinking for us. It is easier to play the game of "Follow the leader" than it is to be a leader. We do not like to make the mental effort necessary to set us apart as an original or independent thinker. This is true in many fields, but it is especially true in the field of religion. We accept without question the ideas presented to us by our ancestors. Martin Luther said, "Any religion that a man has not made for himself is a superstition and not a religion."

Society as a whole does not like to be bothered with new ideas. When someone presents a new idea, the mass mind immediately challenges with the statement, "It can't be done." Of course you know what happens next—someone proceeds to do it!

A steamboat was once an original thought in someone's mind; an airplane was once a much-scoffed-at idea. Because we have had men who took the responsibility of thinking and acting on their own initiative, regardless of the approval or disapproval of the masses, we are today much further along the path of progress than we would have been. It takes men of independence and perseverance to develop the ideas.

Children should be taught the value of self-reliance. A mother who gives her children something definite to do, and makes them individually responsible for that thing, not only helps to develop character in the children but succeeds in keeping a much better-regulated home than she could without their cooperation.

In a well-ordered home each child knows his part in the plan; he is taught the value of service at an early age. He will not grow up under the illusion that he can get what he wants without paying the price. In fact, a child who earns spending money through doing those little odd jobs that help to keep the home in order and harmony can easily appreciate the relation his services bear to acquiring spending money for things he desires. Having had the responsibility of earning his own money, he soon learns to take the responsibility of spending wisely.

Contrast a home in which the children have been taught neither the value nor the necessity of any cooperation on their part. The mother, being spasmodic in her disciplinary methods, attracts spasmodic obedience from the children. One finds her scolding and fussing because Harry or Mary do not respond to her wishes. Unwashed breakfast dishes, unmade beds, and faultfinding and complaining are all evidence that something is radically wrong. No one could enjoy living in this chaotic condition. If children are not taught the value of industry, honesty, and self-reliance at home, they have to build these qualities into their character through hard experience later in life.

No matter in what position one finds himself, he can improve that condition if he wishes to. Abraham Lincoln's opportunities when he was a boy were so meager that not one person in a thousand under similar circumstances would have tried to educate himself. If he had felt, as many persons do who have much better advantages, that he did not have a chance, America would have suffered for lack of the inspiration given through one of her greatest statesmen. Lincoln held himself responsible for an education, not his parents.

Most of us tend to hold the other person responsible. We all like to have someone else to lay the blame on if things do not go well with us. We occasionally hear people say that they have not had a chance to get an education and they are not even trying to help themselves. Think of it in this time of night schools, correspondence schools, lecture courses, and good libraries!

The men who have succeeded in business are the ones who have been willing to think, to plan, and to give the best that was in them to the firms by which they were employed. Had they been too selfish to help where they were, they would never have reached any great measure of success. The persons who succeed are the ones who are not only willing to do what they are paid to do, but more than that. A man who limits his capacity to serve by the size of his pay check never can get beyond small things.

There are individuals in almost every business whose attitude is: "My work does not concern me. I'm just here to earn my living."

Perhaps you have heard the story of the young man who went to his boss to ask why another young man in the firm had been promoted ahead of him. The boss told him to go out and see how many cars of lumber were on the track to be shipped. He soon came back and said, "There are nine cars." He was next asked to see what kind of lumber was in each car. He again went out and came back with this information. He then was asked where it was to be shipped. He went again and came back with this correct answer. Each time he came back he knew just the answer to the direct question. The boss then sent for the other young man and asked him the same question he had asked the first young man. When this young man came back he gave all the information desired, without having to be sent back a number of times. It is easy to see which one had initiative and foresight and which one lacked these qualities.

Promotions come to the one who will assume responsibility, who will see things through. There are always good reasons why one individual fails and the other succeeds. These reasons are not due to anything outside of the individual. It is not because one is oppressed and downtrodden by someone and the other one has "pull." Anyone who springs to the occasion and enters wholeheartedly into doing the thing which is to be done will succeed. The successful person acts, while the one next to him wonders what there will be in it for him.

Independence, happiness, and contentment are the rewards of the individual who is self-reliant. This quality may not at this moment belong to all of us, but it can be developed, if we do not surrender to inertia and indifference.

There is a class of people who are willing to take the responsibility for their successes but not for their failures. When such a person is successful he feels exalted and happy. He feels that he is of great importance and he is willing to assume full responsibility for his success. However, when failure comes into his world he would rather think that God brought it about, or at least that some power outside himself brought it about.

The responsibility for conditions in one's life can be fixed only with the individual. That is the greatest lesson we have to learn. When things go wrong we always feel that it is the other person who is to blame. The people with whom we live or those with whom we are associated cannot be the cause of inharmony in our world. We need to search ourself in order to find what is wrong. We cannot shift the responsibility. Faultfinding and discontent will not get us any place. We must be willing to face our own shortcomings and then work to overcome them. We cannot and will not then be held down.

Saint Bernard says, "Nothing can work me damage except myself; the harm that I sustain I carry about with me, and never am a real sufferer but by my own fault."

We are trying to develop a better civilization, and our success depends first upon the individual and then upon his relation to the group. Individuals as a group go to make up a nation.

Instead of saying, "It is not my fault!" when something goes wrong in your home or office, set about to remedy the condition. Do all in your power to adjust conditions.

Do not be fearful of being censured by someone else, even if you do make a mistake. You will at least have developed in character through having tried.

As intelligent, thinking people we should be willing to be held accountable for the results of our acts. We should not say, "I was told to do that," or, "It was not my fault." We will become more efficient, more capable, and trustworthy when we assume our responsibility toward life.

The Divine Plan for Your Life

There is a wonderful, beautiful plan for your life. Your destiny is divine! As your consciousness of the Christ indwelling is quickened through daily prayer, you find yourself fitting into the divine plan easily. You come to know that you are a part of a great universal plan of spiritual growth and unfoldment.

When you enter into the feeling that you are a part of the good of the world, you are at ease. Frustration vanishes. You live your life in harmony. A hymn in *Unity Song Selections* expresses this thought:

"We are a part of all that's good,
    And good shall be victorious."

You are eternally a part of the good in the world. Know this and be at peace. All is working well in your life and affairs because you are a part of the divine plan for good for every man.

Relax. Be at ease. There is no need to struggle hard to find the good. You are a part of all that is good!

Thoughts
about Special Times

Your Most Fulfilling Gift

Christmas represents the fullness of our joy in giving, in loving, and in serving.

We celebrate Christmas, first because this season gave us Jesus Christ. In giving Jesus Christ to the world, God expressed the fullness of all that He is.

Jesus, as the beloved Son of God, came to show you and me what is in every man. The apostle Paul, our great teacher, showed us clearly what Jesus intended us to know when he said that Jesus was revealing the mystery hidden for ages: "Christ in you, the hope of glory."

So while we are intent upon celebrating Christmas with our loving, giving, and sharing, let us not fail to arouse our own Christ nature. Let us give thanks that this great mystery is revealed to each one of us, and that through this nature within us, we can really give life, joy, love, and hope to the world.

Any gift or revelation must be used in order to be of any help. The Christ aroused within us gives freely and lovingly and generously to others. In our Christmas giving, there is a great void and emptiness unless we give from the heart of love.

If you do not desire to give a gift, give from the heart

of love. Often the one who would receive from you will appreciate your love and blessing and good will as much as receiving an actual gift.

At Christmastime make a special gift to yourself—a gift of a high consciousness attained through prayer. You will then find yourself entering into the real spirit of Christmas. The significance of Christmas in its spiritual value will be revealed. The real spirit felt at Christmas is the spirit of love felt not only for your special friends and your family but for all whom you meet.

Let joy and happiness radiate through you during this season to make others happy. So much of the world celebrates Christmas that it can be a real period of unity and understanding, a time of feeling your unity with all mankind.

Let us make the revelation of the apostle Paul that Christ is in every man, the basis for a meeting place in our hearts with all people of the world. We all want to live in a peaceful world, and this is the time to let the Christ quality of love, which is within every man, come into expression. An expression of love coming directly through the Christ in us will uplift and bless the entire world.

Let us make this Christmas real by putting ourselves into all that it stands for in love and understanding.

Take some special time during your Christmas celebrations to remember to extend your love to the whole world. We all are in this world together to make it a better place in which to live. Let the glory of the Lord shine in your heart and through you to brighten the world.

An Easter Blessing

Everyone loves spring, which comes forth with such freshness and beauty. In our thinking we associate spring and the glory of Easter.

Easter is symbolical of the new life that can be ours. Jesus' resurrection from the tomb shows the tremendous urge of the new life of God to come forth in man. Jesus knew enough about His own spiritual nature to cooperate with it in resurrecting His body.

The same urge for the expression of new life is in you and me. We need to awaken and to cooperate with this urge within us.

We are all receptive to the beauty all about us, yet we sometimes fail to find the beauty within ourself. Jesus Christ came to show us the way to new life. "I came that they may have life, and have it abundantly." We accept Jesus at His word, and lay hold on the new life and the new beginning that are awaiting us.

When we accept the idea of new life in our consciousness, as a next step the idea springs forth in the body, which we recognize as the temple of the living God. We further awaken to the glory of the Christ in our own soul. The Christ has been there all the time, but we are resurrecting it through our thinking. We follow the admonition:

"Arise, shine; for your light has come,
        and the glory of the Lord has risen upon you."

Let us keep this glory within us glowing. It will change our life into a more glorious expression and will charge our body with newness of life. It will charge our affairs with new growth. It will bring all our relationships into harmony and order.

We will come to the realization, "I am a new being in Christ."

One of my favorite prayers is based on these words of Jesus: *"I am the resurrection and the life."* I add further: *"And I rise triumphant out of every trial."* I realize that Christ in me exalts me and lifts me up from any thought of defeat or failure.

Use this prayer: *"I am the resurrection and the life, and I rise triumphant out of every trial."* You will find yourself experiencing the glory of the resurrected Christ within yourself, and your life and affairs will take on this glory.

Accept the Glory of Easter

Easter, the season of resurrection, is at hand, offering us unlimited inspiration to revive our ideals, to lift up our vision of ourself and others, to renew our awareness of the good and beautiful. Now is the perfect time to reach past the darkness, the humiliation, the scars, and accept the joy of the Lord. As a child welcomes the dawn with a heart filled with expectation and hope, let us welcome Easter, the symbol of light.

All about us now we sense nature's awakening. We see bleak fields turning green. We notice that the winds have grown soft and fragrant. The skies, once gray and threatening, have lightened. Though the ground be packed hard, we see crocuses pressing through to the light. I wonder, as I look at them, if there is any obstacle great enough to hold us back when we have this same inner urge to press out into the light, to grow, to expand, to increase in usefulness.

As the warm rays of the sun are stirring all nature to life, so the inspiration of the Easter season is arousing in us a desire to push up and out of our present limitations to a sweeter, stronger expression of ourself.

A song of sunshine through the rain,
    Of spring across the snow;
A balm to heal the hurts of pain,
    A peace surpassing woe.
Lift up your heads, ye sorrowing ones,
    And be ye glad of heart,
For Calvary and Easter Day

Were just three days apart!

The remembrance of that wondrous morn when our Lord Christ triumphed over death stirs in us a deeper confidence in the divinity of man and his ability to free himself from every Calvary. The remembrance of His great courage and faith awakens in us a determination to revive all the high ideals that we have ever cherished in our heart.

This is the season of new life, of growth, of new expression. This is the perfect time to revive our ideals, to lift up our vision, to acknowledge our own at-one-ment with God, all good.

This is the season of rejoicing, of light, of resurrection.

"Sing, soul of mine, this day of days.
        The Lord is risen.
Toward the sunrising set thy face.
        The Lord is risen.
Behold He giveth strength and grace;
For darkness, light; for mourning, praise;
For sin, His holiness; for conflict, peace.
Arise, O soul, this Easter Day!
Forget the tomb of yesterday,
For thou from bondage art set free;
Thou sharest in His victory
And life eternal is for thee,
Because the Lord is risen."

Vacation Time

I feel that a vacation, whether taken at home or in some faraway place, is an opportunity for renewal and refreshment. It is a good time to lift our thinking from the daily regular duties, a time to shake off any limitations we have placed upon ourself, a time to get a larger view of ourself and our world.

When I go on a vacation, I let my vision expand to include a different world into which I must fit myself. I expect new and joyous experiences along the way. I feel that all the people whom I meet are my friends. If I am traveling with a group, it is surely a time to express harmony, love, and understanding. There is nothing so unpleasant as traveling with a disgruntled companion. So I try constantly to expand my own loving feeling toward everyone and to have a sense of peace within myself.

If one needs to overcome negative moods, vacation time is a good time to do this. We can decide to be an improved person by the time our vacation is over. This attitude of self-improvement will be felt not only in our own good health and happiness but in our relations with others.

Vacation time is also an opportunity to do some special things for our wonderful body. I think of taking walks, of getting good fresh air and needed physical exercise. This is the time to do some of the things we haven't had time for in our regular routine.

When you leave home on a vacation, be sure to bless your home and your relatives. Place everything in

God's hands and leave with a peaceful heart. Then don't keep thinking about what you have left behind. Take advantage of your time to enjoy new things, new persons, and happy and rich experiences.

The following are ideas that you can take with you to think about and work on as you drive along the highway, as you fly in an airplane, as you walk in a forest:

I am a part of all the good there is in the world.

God is so wonderful, life is so beautiful, and I am so richly blessed.

I am young, strong, vital, healthy. My body accepts these ideas and responds to them.

I am uplifted and joyous all day long.

Wherever I am, God is. His presence guides, directs, and sustains me.

God is my refuge and my strength. Beneath me are the everlasting arms, and love divine is over all.

September Reminder

This season of the year finds many of us returning to some special study. Children, of course, are returning to their schools; and many adults are starting classwork or specialized study of some particular subject.

It is well for us who are doing this to consider the Source of our intelligence, the Source of our wisdom and understanding. The all-knowing Mind of God, in the midst of each of us, is this source. Therefore, when we turn to this Mind, we think clearly, understand easily, and express readily.

In understanding that we have the Mind of God in us from which we draw, we can say often and with faith, *"My mind is alert, keen, and perfect in expression."* We can say of ourself, *"I know, I remember, I understand. I express myself perfectly."*

Let us rejoice that our mind is flexible and alert. Let us rejoice that we comprehend readily and put right instruction into action quickly. Let us rejoice that we learn easily.

Worldwide Prayer

There is great harmony and understanding between the seekers of the light in all countries of the world, and truly the seekers of the light are one. And together we are bringing light and healing to the world.

People Are Praying around the World

On a tour around the world I was inspired by the praying people I met. In the temples of Japan, Bangkok, in India, and in the mosques of Egypt there were always people praying.

Between praying people there is a bond of feeling. Our ways of prayer are different, but we are all seeking the same source of wisdom, understanding, inspiration, and right answers in order to enjoy living. Instinctive in all mankind is the need to come up higher.

Our Unity representative in Japan, Mr. Ide, is a member of the International Interfaith Fellowship. When I reached Kyoto, the International Interfaith group in that city called my hotel to see if I would have lunch with them. There were eight of the group present, with an interpreter, Mr. Kurukara. These men were all outstanding in the religious field in Japan.

After lunch I suggested that I would like to see the special shrines where they were teaching and leading meditations.

One of these men took me to Itzo Ken, which means "The Garden of Light." Here I met a Buddist priest who was carrying *Lessons in Truth* under his arm!

Mr. Osado, of Chicago, a Japanese who has been in the United States for many years, had copies of *Lessons in Truth* printed in Japanese and sent them all over Japan. It was one of these copies the priest had gotten hold of. I have a picture of him carrying it under his arm. He prized it highly. The receptivity of the Japanese to Unity is very wonderful.

Mr. Kurukara told me that he would be in Osaka on Sunday night and would pick me up at the hotel and take me to Mr. Miyake's temple. At the hour when he was to pick me up I almost wished I had not accepted this offer. We had traveled from early morning and had taken in so many sights in Koyoto that at seven in the evening I had just reached the hotel.

But there to meet me was Mr. Kurukara with Mr. Miyake, the temple minister, and they came in a car driven by a chauffeur.

I did not have a chance to change my traveling clothes, but went as I was. When we reached the temple there were several hundred people, all sitting on the floor, and they were chanting the most powerful chant I had ever heard.

Of course, we took off our shoes when we entered the building. Mr. Miyake took us into his study where they served fruit and tea and little cakes. After talking for about a half hour through the interpreter, we were taken into the temple.

I put my shoes on again as they all did. Then I forgot to take them off when we entered the temple. They had put chairs for us up front, and I scooted my shoes under my chair.

On both sides of the platform there were musicians, about twenty on either side, all robed in white.

I had just sat down when Mr. Kurukara said that Mr. Miyake would like for me to go to the platform after he returned to his place, and do exactly as he did.

For a moment I felt entirely alone in a very strange world. There was no one there I knew.

However, I watched Mr. Miyake very carefully and when he returned to his chair, I asked God to go with me. You see, in Unity we do not have any forms or ceremony, and this was all new and strange to me.

I went to the altar, carrying a little bouquet which they handed me. I got down on my knees before the altar, bowed toward it twice, then stood and did this again. Then I clapped my hands three times, as Mr. Miyake had done.

Then, as he had done, I backed away from the altar, facing the altar until I got off the platform.

Later on I was asked to talk for ten minutes. Mr. Kurukara interpreted what I said. The people present applauded very happily, still on their knees.

None of the other members of the group I was traveling with had felt equal to going to the temple after our long day's trip, but it was the experience of a lifetime, and one I shall always remember.

In Bangkok, where the golden-robed priests gathered together in their temple on their knees, I also found a bond of love and unity.

In every country we visited there were shrines and temples and churches. In Spain the church is nowadays more like a museum. But the spirit in which it was originally constructed is still alive and a blessing to many people. People need and want a feeling of unity with other praying people.

There is great harmony and understanding between the seekers of the light in all countries of the world, and truly "the seekers of the light are one." Together we are bringing light and healing to the world.

Take Part in the Peace !

We are citizens of the world, and we have a part to play in bringing about right and just conditions in all the earth. We know that a righteous and just peace is for the good of the whole world, and we pray that great and understanding world leaders may come forth, those with love in their hearts for all humanity. We pray also that all international leaders may be guided and directed and inspired to do those things that are right for humanity.

Let us pray for our own leaders in governmental affairs, asking that they be inspired, guided, directed; that through the Christ Mind we may be united in thought and purpose for the good of our country. Then let us pray further that the leaders of all the nations of the earth may also be united in thought and purpose for the good of all humanity. Thus we take part in the peace, thus we promote unity in the world!

"Through the Christ Mind we are unified in thought and purpose for the good of all humanity."

Questions and Answers

The following section consists of questions and answers covering practically every point of Truth and its application to human life and affairs.

May Rowland answered these questions spontaneously during Healing-Prayer Workshops, which are a part of every Unity Village Retreat. Even though many of the answers are brief, we feel that you will find them extremely helpful.

Questions and Answers About Human Relations

How can one best adjust to the passing of a mate?

Too many people withdraw into a shell of grief and loneliness. We may have to make a real effort to become interested in other people, and to show this interest. If a person prays about it he will be shown how to extend his interest to include others. Many times a person feels led to join some kind of service organization or to do some kind of voluntary work. But everywhere there are people who need understanding, people who need someone just to talk to them or to listen to them. We are helped in our efforts to make a new life for ourselves as we try to help others find more happiness in their lives.

I have recently remarried and I have a son and a daughter who have come to live with me. They have lived with my former wife a long time and they seem to resent this change and my life style, etc.

I think that by continually radiating love and asking for wisdom and good judgment in all your dealings with these children, you will be able to handle this situation. Everyone responds to love, eventually. It may take a little while for the children to accept this situation and to feel that you truly love them. But as you persist in being loving and harmonious and do not respond to their negative attitudes, you will soon win them over. Don't be discouraged if this takes a little time. These children will soon think you are as wonderful as you are.

What about my son or daughter who uses drugs or smokes pot?

It takes a tremendous amount of patience to heal some of these young people who have gotten into these habits. But I think that with patience we can help them work it out. These young people are all seeking something and sometimes they don't know just what. They are seeking experiences that satisfy. They have had experiences that didn't satisfy. The search for satisfaction is really a soul hunger. The only thing that will satisfy this hunger is to awaken to one's spiritual nature. We need to understand that these young people are reaching out for something. We need much patience, understanding, prayer, and wise counsel if we are going to help these young people. We should pray for their freedom, their wisdom, their guidance and direction.

Then we have to free them. We can't make anyone do what we want him to do, but sometimes parents make this mistake. They think that because they are the parents and older and wiser they should be able to tell their children what to do. But we can't force things on anyone. Every individual is a free soul. We can pray for him. That is the best thing we can do for him, to pray for him in the understanding that he is a child of God, that all the longings of his soul will be satisfied as he comes to know his spiritual nature. There is a right and perfect outworking for his life, there is a way that will bring him happiness and good. We need to keep praying and holding him in that consciousness.

We hear all the time about young people who are gaining their freedom from drugs and negative approaches to life. Our prayers should always be for another's freedom from any kind of bondage. We should pray that his desires will be divinely directed and that in his reaching out he will find that which is for his growth and development and soul unfoldment. This is the way I look at it. We should keep praying for any young person who needs help and never give up on him.

Why is a person very kind and loving and then the next moment very cruel and spiteful?

Many people act this way. Rather than getting upset, it is best to overlook it, and not to judge by appearances. We should always pray for the other person. And our prayer should always be for his illumination. As we pray for illumination for others and also for ourself, we will try to understand what makes another person act the way he does. As we hold to the idea of the constructive, harmonizing, unifying power of love we will be blessed and we will be a blessing. Really, this is a healing need; if we think of it in this way, we will not be upset and we will be able to be of help through our loving prayer.

Does one learn to accept undesirable habits of a loved one, or should he try to change them?

One shouldn't nag or find fault, but pray for the other's light and understanding and overcoming. Behold the Christ. Know for a dear one that God satisfies his longing soul and fills his life with good.

How can I pray for someone who is a slave to a possessive mother?

Pray for his strength and freedom from bondage. See him unfettered and unbound, free spirit. Also pray for the mother. Sometimes bondage is the fault of the possessed, and they both need to be freed.

My problem is that I have given my whole life to my family. Now I am needed only as a baby-sitter or when they want to borrow money.

A person should not sell himself out to anybody. You are an individual soul. You shouldn't lose contact with other people. You need to keep in touch with life and expand your own consciousness. Don't feel lonely or sorry for yourself. It is up to each one of us to make a life. Decide that you are going to do something about it. People have started a whole new life for themselves after their family has grown and gone on their own. Give your family your love and blessing and release them.

How can a wife be more loving to her husband and help bring peace to home and children?

She can work on expressing the quality of love. We have to let love express itself through us. We can learn to radiate love not just when things are pleasant but all the time. One person in a family can inaugurate good. We sometimes forget to express love toward family members. Even when we do not like what someone does, we can love him. That's the time we need most of all to express love.

What if the one who prays for right companionship attracts the wrong person? Now how does he pray?

This reminds me of what Mr. Fillmore said once. He told about a woman who had prayed for six months to get a husband and it took her six years to get rid of him. So I would say that it is better to pray for right companionship rather than to pray specifically for a man.

Should we teach our children to take care of themselves, to put their coats on, or their overshoes? Or should we tell them that the Lord will take care of them?

You must use common sense. To believe that the Lord takes care of us does not mean that we do not have to use our heads. If it is cold and snowy, put the children's coats on. However, if they should go out without them, don't be afraid that they will take cold. They won't.

Would it be possible to pray to attract a husband or wife to oneself?

You attract into your life what you need. Ask for wisdom and good judgment and right companionship. Learn to be loving toward all people and to be outgoing. We never attract others if we are closed in and limit our expression of love. One of the favorite Unity affirmations is: *"I am a radiating center of divine love, mighty to attract my good and to radiate good to others."* To this a person might add, *"And I attract into my life right companionship."*

It is always right to pray for the right companionship. If this is your desire, talk to God. Tell Him your need. Affirm that the way is open for you to have a happy life and right companionship.

Sometimes when people pray for companionship they decide in their minds just the kind of person this has to be. If a woman is praying for a man she may decide he has to have certain kind of hair, or job, or other characteristics. I think one should ask for right companionship, and then trust God to bring the right answer to you.

How can one find a more rewarding and meaningful life in middle age?

Most people begin to seek spiritual answers in middle age. They should also seek to be more outgoing. Friendly people attract interesting and happy experiences. If we do not feel naturally outgoing, it helps to take an affirmation such as, *"I love all people and all people love me."* To really love people makes you free and at one with all people.

Anyone who wants a more rewarding and meaningful life can find it. There are always ways to broaden our life, to expand it. We may need to make room for friends, we may need to take part in life and not just sit on the sidelines and watch life go by.

Questions and Answers About Practicing Truth

If I live positively and affirm Truth regularly, and pray daily, should I expect any negative things in my life?

You shouldn't expect negative things. But neither should you expect to be free from any challenging experiences. This is how we grow. We do not rise all at once into the Christ consciousness. It is a gradual development; it is a process of unfoldment. And we learn and grow through our experiences.

Why can I not have a life free of problems?

The astronauts would never have walked on the moon but for some of the setbacks. In meeting problems, we develop spiritual strength and power. Man is not an underling; he is meant to overcome and to conquer.

Do you believe one can change the pattern of his life through right thinking?

Yes, anyone can. The whole pattern of life can change through the daily practice of positive, constructive thinking. Many people tell us that their whole life is changed through reading *Daily Word* day by day and incorporating these ideas into their daily living. We in Silent Unity begin our day with *Daily Word* and find that to do so helps us to keep our thoughts and feelings harmonious and in tune with God's good.

What do you mean by the light touch?

I like the idea of giving things the light touch. We dramatize so much negation and talk about it and make a big thing of it instead of letting it pass and giving it the light touch. When people want to tell you about all the hardships they have ever heard about, not only their own but everyone else's, I always say: "Give it the light touch. Let it go. Don't make something out of it. Don't dramatize the negative side of life."

The idea of giving things the light touch came to me very clearly one time when I needed it. It was on a Friday afternoon and I was very busy. We were about to close the office and word came that one of our workers had passed away. She didn't have any relatives or anyone to attend to things and it was up to me to make the arrangements for her service and take charge of everything in relation to it. For the moment it seemed too much for me, and I thought, "What am I going to do about this?" It was just as though I had a tap on the shoulder and something said, "Give it the light touch!" So I did just that; I gave it the light touch. I was guided to ask just the right persons to help handle things and everything worked out in order. I personally couldn't have worked out these things. I have learned that one must not bear down on problems or think of them as hard. Some people make such hard work out of the things that they are called on to do. We can learn, no matter what we have to meet, to give it the light touch.

One time in the Silent Unity work when our mail was extremely heavy and we did not seem to be able to handle it, we asked Mr. Fillmore to pray with us. Charles Fillmore told us not to be concerned, to go back to our work and to bless every letter with this thought: *"Jesus Christ has healed you. Jesus Christ has prospered you";* to know that whatever the need, the answer was already there. It was marvelous the way the mail moved. We were giving it the light touch. And we had more wonderful reports of healings.

Can you give assurance to one who is learning to overcome fear?

There is nothing to fear. "God has not given us a spirit of fear, but of power and of love and of a sound mind." Take an affirmation such as: *"There is nothing to fear. God is love, and God is with me."* You can establish these ideas in your mind so that they become part of you and you will find that fear is no longer part of you. You can build in fearlessness. A psychologist once said, "If you take to your heels, fears usually will take to theirs." In other words, if we do not allow ourself to be paralyzed by fear but get busy and active doing something constructive, fear usually disappears.

What is a good affirmation for the correct use of time?

We might take an affirmation such as *"The Christ Mind directs me in using my time wisely and well."* As I use my time wisely and well there is no hurry, no anxiety, no push to get things done. There is an order about it. Another good affirmation is, *"Divine order is established in the use of my time."* If we feel hurried we don't accomplish much. So if we can know that we are in divine order and that everything in our life moves in harmony and order, we will find that we have time enough to do all that needs to be done. Time is a man-made concept that we allow to limit us. When we get our thinking straight, when we are orderly in our thinking and in our habits, then we will be on time, we will be where we should be, at the right time. And we won't feel pushed or rushed. We all have to work on this idea of time, because there are so many things that we have to do and to accomplish.

One of the confusing things about the Unity teachings to some people is the statement "There is no evil," when we know there is evil all around us.

Evil is an appearance that we know has to be changed and can be changed. We bless all appearances, even the ones that seem evil, and have faith that good can be brought forth out of them. When we say there is no evil, we are saying, "There is no power in evil." We may have given it power by our thoughts, but we can change this through changing our thinking.

How can one forgive himself for past mistakes?

Accept the forgiving love of Jesus Christ. It doesn't make any difference what the mistake has been; the forgiving love of Jesus Christ sets you free. Affirm: *"The forgiving love of Jesus Christ sets me free from all mistakes of the past."*

How do you get joy in living?

Start with affirmative prayer. Take an idea such as *"The joy of the Lord uplifts and blesses me all day long."* Joy is a wellspring within you and will respond to your word.

I seem to get in turmoil over my work. Can you give me an affirmation?

When things are in a turmoil, what is needed is divine order. Take an affirmation such as, *"Divine order is established in my mind, in my thinking."* This is where divine order starts, not in your affairs but in your mind, in your thinking. Then affirm: *"Divine order is expressed through all my affairs. Everything I do is in divine order."*

How can one find what one is really meant to do in life after the children are grown and one is left all alone?

Take this thought, *"I resolve to let the will of God be done in my life and affairs."* Think of what you want and put it into words, into positive form. Resolve to let the perfect will of God work through you, and have the courage to follow the inspiration that comes.

Does God have a plan for me?

There is a divine plan for each one of us. It unfolds through us. We do not always see what this plan is, but we are growing. We should ask for wisdom each day to know what the divine plan is for us.

How can we really know what our goal in life is?

Say: "God, You show me. Reveal the right path to me." The wisdom of God directs you.

Unity says that regardless of what happens, we are to pronounce it good. How can I do this? What does "Pronounce it good" mean?

This is a way of looking at every experience, even the ones that seem hard or difficult. No matter how tragic a circumstance may be, some good will come out of it. If, no matter what the appearance, we can look at it and say to ourself, "I pronounce it good," we open the way for the good to come forth. The good is there, even though we don't always see it. We keep ourself from being overcome by circumstances as we have the faith to pronounce them good, and as we hold fast to the idea that the power of God is at work. Sometimes it takes time and perspective to be able to see that some situation was really for good. But we may be sure that God is working in and through all things and that good will be forthcoming.

How can Unity make greater impact on world government? It seems to me that Unity principles are a wonderful way to personal serenity, but there continues to be injustice and such world disorder that I feel that much more could be done on a national and world level.

We hope to have more effect on these conditions. We are praying every day for world conditions and have been for years. We have faith that these world conditions can be worked out, that order, harmony, and understanding can be brought forth. Of course, this takes growth on the part of a great number of people. We feel that our part is to pray for world conditions every day, no matter what the appearance is, and we do.

Questions and Answers
About Man as a Spiritual Being

What is meant when we say that man is a spiritual being?

The Spirit in us transcends our personal self. We need to think of the transcendent power in us. What we put into our consciousness is important. We can identify ourself with that which is less than we are; or we can identify ourself with the Truth about us, which is that we are a spiritual being. A helpful affirmation to remember is, *"I transcend myself and all my affairs, for I am Spirit."*

You are getting younger every day. How do you do it?

Well, I don't talk about age. Mr. Fillmore started telling his age when he got up in his nineties. I asked him one time: "Why do you brag about your age? You always told us not to talk about years or how long we have been here." He said, "I wish I had never started telling my age." He taught us that we shouldn't talk about age. He said: "Don't pile years on yourself. How long you have lived is not important. You've been here for eternity and you will be here through eternity."

One time a guide was conducting a tour through the Unity buildings. He was asked, "How old is Lowell Fillmore?" The guide said he didn't know. Then he was asked, "How old is May Rowland?" The guide said,

"I'll ask and find out." When he came to me with this question, I said, "I have been here throughout eternity and I expect to stay."

When you bear down on age you add to your consciousness all the decrepit ideas that are associated with age. You don't want to let these ideas take over. If you begin to say you are old, then you are sure to follow through in the way you look and feel. Your wonderful body listens to what you say. If you keep saying: "I'm getting old. I'm tired," what do you expect your body to do? If you talk about being young and happy and full of good years, you will feel this kind of response in your body. Many psychologists are discovering that the more a person talks about age the older he feels. You don't want to pile up years on yourself. You want to build up wonderful, beautiful, vital ideas that help you to enjoy life.

How do you feel about living forever?

I feel that there is the possibility of eternal life. We just haven't reached it.

Are you going to make it?

Sometime. I won't say when.

Would you explain the difference between spirit and soul?

Spirit is the presence of God within you and soul is the repository of all your experiences in all your life.

114

The remembrance of everything that ever comes into your experience is the remembrance of your soul. You are spirit, soul, and body.

Do you believe in spirit communication?

I believe in communication with the one Spirit, the Spirit of God within us.

I don't believe that we ever get any special good from communication with someone who has left this life and doesn't know any more than we do. Usually this is what is meant by spirit communication—the attempt to communicate with someone who has passed out of the body.

The one Spirit, God, the Holy Spirit, the Spirit of Truth is always with you, and you can always communicate with this Spirit and find guidance and right answers.

The Bible states that every man must surrender to Christ in order to be born anew. How does one have the nerve to walk that gangplank?

When we are willing to let God take over, when we surrender self-will, then we establish something eternal in our consciousness. Our willingness to let God's will be done makes a path for us.

We can say to ourself, "I am willing to let God's perfect will be done in my life." Surrender doesn't necessarily take courage. When we surrender to God we are surrendering to the good, to the positive. It isn't hard work. Sometimes the personal will may get us into trouble. Asking that the will of Christ in the midst of you be fulfilled makes your life a joyous experience. You are never off the track, you are continually brought back to the Truth of your being.

Are we bound by karma or can we learn in other ways?

The belief in karma says that if you make a mistake you must work out the results of that mistake in some other incarnation. But we believe that the forgiving love of Jesus Christ can wipe out the mistakes of the past.

This is one of our principles. We accept the forgiving love of this wonderful Christ. The Christ is in you. This spirit frees you from the bondage of past mistakes. You don't have to be bound to the past. I think the difference between the idea of the Christ forgiveness and that of karma is that those who believe in karma think that they have to go on, lifetime after lifetime, working out the sins and mistakes they make along the way. We don't accept this concept. We feel that anybody can be free who will accept the principles of Truth and the principles of forgiveness. Through the grace of God in every man, forgiveness can come.

I frequently say to myself, "The forgiving love of Christ sets me free from the mistakes of the past and the results of mistakes of the past." This frees the subconscious mind. You see, we carry in the subconscious mind the memories of past mistakes and we have to give them up and get rid of them.

Questions and Answers About Death, Reincarnation

I am uncertain as to what to do with my life. I recently lost my husband. I am so alone. Can you tell me what I can do to find my way?

We all know persons who have adjusted to great loss and change in their lives. It takes work. But we should not close ourself in. Make new friends. Try to do something that will help other persons. Don't keep yourself behind closed doors. A person can't just sit in his grief and feel sorry for himself. Try to do something useful and something helpful, and be an outgoing person. You have to take some action. Every person knows something he can do to change his life.

I have a prayer that I love: *"God works in me and through me to enrich and expand my life."* Let the good come. Don't shut it out because of a feeling of unhappiness. This is the attitude we have to take. We have to go on living our life and unfolding and growing. There are so many people who need help, and a person who has even a small concept of Truth can give it out to others.

I had an operation and the doctors gave no hope, but I was healed. A dear friend had the same experience; she too had Silent Unity prayer, and she passed on. Why?

We cannot answer why one person proves the law

117

and another doesn't. One person may be more receptive. Some persons do not really want to be well. But the answer is in the soul. No one else can know another's soul experiences. We have to know that each one is following through on the pattern that is for his highest good. Why a person doesn't respond to prayer is something in his own soul. The soul contains the answer to "Why?" We should not say that the person who passes on didn't have faith. We don't know. The answer is between him and his indwelling Lord. There it has to stay. He can't tell it to me or anybody else, but the answer is there.

Will I meet my loved ones again?

I think this depends on many things. It will probably be determined by what we need in our next experience. But I have no doubt that we are brought together with those we love.

There is no separation in love. We are always one with God and one with those we love. We attract the situations and people that belong to us. We may be drawn together again with someone we loved dearly. But we need to remember that we are related to all people in a bond of oneness and unity.

What do we say to parents whose child passes on, even though he was prayed for?

The theory of reincarnation sometimes seems to offer the only answer. We have to believe that life never ends. Jesus said, "I go to prepare a place for you." We believe that He meant by this, to prepare a place in consciousness.

In the case of the child, we cannot say why he did not respond to prayer, but we can hold to the idea of the continuity of life. The soul will be reincarnated and go on to fulfill its destiny.

Reincarnation is also an answer to the question as to why a child is born deformed, and so on. This span of life is not the only life. Life is eternal.

I told my daughter to know that she was protected. She said that I said the same thing to her husband who was killed in an accident a year ago.

I had a nephew who was drowned at the age of nineteen, trying to save a girl's life. "Why, why, why?" kept ringing through my mind and his parents' minds. Francis J. Gable at the funeral service said, "Sometimes a person fulfills his mission while very young."

Unity believes that life is eternal, that though we may not always be in the same body, we are a living soul forever. We have many experiences and grow through them. Even in a close human relationship, we have to know that this soul is a child of God, and if he passes on, release him and know that wherever he is, God is.

Every day you must get letters from people whose prayers are not answered. How do you reply to some-one who says, for instance: "I was praying for my son's safety and he was killed. I feel there is no God"?

Of course, we have to deal with the faith of that

person. He probably hasn't lost all faith in God, but he has lost faith as far as the son is concerned. Even when a person passes on, the prayers that have been said in his behalf have done him some good. Prayer takes hold in the soul. All prayer is good, and there is some kind of answer to every prayer. It may not be just the answer we are looking for, but still a blessing is given.

There are hundreds of persons whom we pray for who come through victoriously. From a human standpoint, we cannot tell why one person is helped and the other one isn't. We believe that life is eternal, that life goes on, that every soul has many opportunities to express and develop his soul consciousness. The more we develop ourself right now, the better it is for us in our next life experience.

Do many people ask, "Why did this happen?" when someone passes on?

Yes, many people ask "Why?" when someone passes. They may say: "He was such a good person. Why did this happen to him?" We always say that this individual was a child of God and that it is not up to us to try to determine why he didn't come through some experience. There are many things in an individual's soul that account for his letting go of life. Sometimes a person doesn't really want to live; another person may want to very much. I think there are forces and energies at work in the individual and the decision is made in him. Usually he is not conscious of this, of course. The decision is between the individual and his own indwelling Lord.

The Lord of his own being knows what he can do. Charles Fillmore, when he was in his nineties, was asked if he would like to go on and prove the truth of eternal life in the body, or if he would be ready to release his body and to reincarnate again. He said, "Well, the Lord of my being won't allow me to go on." He felt within himself that he didn't have the understanding to take the full step. But he made great progress in his overcoming. At one time he was sure that he was going to make the grade. And scientists now are telling us that perpetual life in the body is not an impossibility.

One of the things that was such a good example to all of us in Unity was Mr. Fillmore's persistence in holding to this idea of healing, even though it seemed as though he didn't get results. He worked for years on healing. And he lived to be ninety-four years old.

Does Unity believe in reincarnation?

We accept reincarnation as a theory. We feel certain that people have many, many opportunities to create a life. Charles Fillmore said that it has taken us two thousand years to understand what Jesus Christ was talking about. We cannot expect to get immediate results about all the things we are trying to accomplish. We are on the way; we are growing and unfolding.

The ultimate goal is to learn the principles of Jesus Christ and to live and have perfect control of the body. We have not reached that place yet. We think of reincarnation as a bridge to cross to the place where we can prove that we are eternal beings. We accept the theory of reincarnation because it answers so many questions.

Sometimes a person will ask: "Why is a child born with a defect? We were good parents and I don't know why this happened." Well, I don't think anyone can answer this question, but reincarnation helps to provide a partial answer at least.

Because we have lived many lives, we have come through many experiences. Eternity is a long, long time. We have been here through eternity and we are going to stay, so we might as well be about the Father's business and learn how to live and enjoy life.

Questions and Answers About Helping Others

What is the best way to help another?

The Spirit of God is in every man; it is in the one you would help. Prayers are directed toward arousing that Spirit. Pray for light and understanding. Every prayer is effective, because it arouses the Spirit of God. This comes about, not through the person who does the praying, but through the Spirit within him. The Spirit of God in you has only one project, *you.* The Spirit in the one for whom you pray has only one project, to bless that one. This is what you are to remember. And when you pray for another, trust the answer to the Spirit within him.

Shouldn't we sympathize with others?

What we want to give others is more than sympathy; it is compassion and understanding. We shouldn't just sympathize with the negative side. We need to see the good, to see others strong and able to meet their needs. We want to speak positive words of Truth and to stay on God's side, the good side.

Are you objective or do you sometimes feel so sorry for someone that you become emotionally involved?

No, I don't allow myself to become emotionally involved. You can't help people if you become bogged down in their problems. This is the time to be strong in the Lord and in the power of His might. If we believe that with God all things are possible, then we never give way to appearances. Appearances can be changed.

The daughter of one of our workers was in an automobile accident last winter. The doctors didn't give her the slightest hope. She was just broken up, crushed. But we prayed with the girl, and she is doing fine. You have to have faith in spite of appearances. Your faith must go higher than appearances.

Can you help heal someone who has a negative attitude? I believe but this person doesn't believe.

Most people have faith to some degree. We always try to help a person get out of his negative state.

Sometimes a person is healed who seems to have no faith. What we remember as we pray is that the Christ is in every man. We always pray for illumination. And we know that faith can be stirred up, that spiritual understanding can be quickened through the power of prayer.

Questions and Answers About Healing

I do not have faith in healing. How can I stir it up?

"Faith comes from what is heard, and what is heard comes by the preaching of Christ." Every time you speak a word of healing, there is a listening quality in you that picks it up. Faith is quickened by your listening to your words of Truth and by meeting in agreement with Truth ideas.

Did Charles and Myrtle Fillmore both realize a healing?

Yes, both of them. Myrtle, as probably you have read, was tubercular, and the doctors had given her just six months to live. Mr. Fillmore took her to Colorado but the condition did not improve, so they returned to Kansas City. The Fillmores heard of some lessons that were being given by a representative of Emma Curtis Hopkins (one of the early-day Truth teachers, who taught many of the great Truth leaders.) In this lecture the idea was brought out that God is the source of our life and that we do not inherit sickness or disease. Mrs. Fillmore felt she had inherited tuberculosis, so this idea struck her forcibly. Right away she commenced to see life differently. She said to herself, "If I didn't inherit disease and if I inherit life from God, my Father, then why should I not be healed!" She was healed in a very short time. Then she started helping others—her neighbors, friends, acquaintances. The news of her healing spread and people began coming to her from everywhere. Mr. Fillmore wasn't caught up in the healing work at first, but he began to be more and more impressed and interested in these Truth ideas. Mr. Fillmore was a deep thinker and studied the Truth from every angle. He began with a great intellectual understanding, which deepened into spiritual vision.

How can a person say "I am not sick," when he obviously is?

The more a person talks and thinks about illness, the stronger is its hold on him. Some people dramatize all the negative things that happen and seem to invite difficult experiences. It has been proved that there is healing power in right thinking, in emphasizing the positive side of things, in proclaiming wholeness and perfection. Persons who find it difficult to say "I am not sick" can still put their thoughts on the positive side. They can proclaim their belief that God has created them for life, which is another way of saying, "I am not sick."

The Unity teaching says that pain, sickness, old age, and so on are not real. How about my rheumatism? It's real enough!

It may be real enough, but it is not a permanent condition and it can be changed and healed.

Does this apply to old age too?

Yes. We need to form the habit of thinking of ourself as eternally young. We need to get rid of old ideas. We are not old, decrepit, weak. We should affirm for ourself that we are spiritually alive, that we are continually renewed and rejuvenated.

What part does forgiveness play in healing?

Many persons keep condemning themselves. This is a block to healing. We can take the idea that the forgiving love of Jesus Christ sets us free from all mistakes of the past. Consciously and subconsciously we need to know this truth. Old thoughts and old conditions are as waters that have passed away. Charles Fillmore gave us this affirmation: *"I no longer accuse myself or others of sin and evil. Forgiving, I am forgiven and healed."* The forgiving love of Jesus Christ reaches to the depths of our being, and we are healed.

If a person is ill, should he see a doctor or should he depend solely on prayer?

This is a matter of individual guidance. We never tell a person that he should or shouldn't see a doctor. If someone writes and asks us if he should, we tell him to pray for guidance and then to follow his own inner leading. We pray with him not only for his healing but that he will know the right steps to take.

Why is it that a person slips back into upset conditions? Is it lack of faith?

It may be lack of faith or it may be lack of persistence. We need to tell ourself, "I am making progress; I am going forward." We shouldn't say, "Yesterday I felt well; today I don't feel so good." This offsets the good. As we keep on keeping on, the body will respond to what we think, say, and do.

Charles Fillmore worked continually with the idea of perfecting his body. At one time in his life he had to wear iron braces, but in later years he walked with scarcely a limp. At ninety four he was strong and healthy. We all need to work along these lines, to know that the body is spiritual in essence. Sometimes we get tired of working with the idea of perfecting the body, but Mr. Fillmore worked at it fifty years.

How do you heal high blood pressure? How do you pray for that?

We need to affirm that the heart is doing its work perfectly and that the organs and functions are in divine order.

I think that sometimes a person needs some outer direction. He may need to be careful of his eating habits. Sometimes persons with high blood pressure are overweight, but not always. I think that if a person with this condition prays about it and asks what is right to do, he will be shown anything he needs to do in the outer to facilitate healing. He may be guided to cut down on his appetite; he may be shown that he needs to free himself from mental tension and concern, all the things that make the heart beat faster.

How can I overcome periodic fatigue?

You need to work on the quality of strength. Relax and affirm strength and power in God. Center your attention in the back. A good, strong affirmation is: *"My strength is the strength of ten thousand! I never grow weak or weary."* We all need strength—spiritual strength, bodily strength. We increase our strength through speaking powerful, strong words. Don't ever say that you are tired, old, rundown. Your body is your audience. It is listening.

I claim that I am receiving healing and give thanks for it, but at the same time I cannot deny the physical pain I am experiencing.

I would like to tell you about Mary Wessel. She is a wonderful woman who has been in the Unity work for many years. Before she came into the Unity work she was quite ill with tuberculosis. She found this Bible text: "Let the weak say, I am strong." She commenced to do just this. She said that these words were for her because she felt so weak she could hardly get around. As she affirmed strength, the idea took hold in her and she was eventually completely healed, just as Myrtle Fillmore was. Mary Wessel was using the power of affirmative prayer. This is the Unity way. We don't beg God to heal us. We affirm life and health. We say: *"The health of God is manifesting itself in me. The life of God is flowing through me."*

Does it do any good to pray for someone for healing

*when he himself does not appear to have any faith and
is not interested in prayer?*

I think that when a person is not interested in prayer
and seems to have no faith, it is more difficult to reach
him. People need to be receptive to spiritual ideas
before they really receive the benefits of prayer; an
open mind is needed.

We are always glad to pray for those who need help,
whether they have any understanding of faith and
prayer or not. But we pray for their illumination, for
their understanding as well as for their healing.

*How do I overcome negative beliefs, such as the
belief that I have a chronic condition?*

We hypnotize ourself with the thought that something is chronic or incurable. We need to build a consciousness of health. Tell yourself that you are strong,
alive, alert, healthy. Affirm that you are strong in mind
and body. Then meet in agreement with these ideas.
Something in you will eventually respond.

Sometimes we just repeat affirmations. We need to
listen to our words, to say to ourself, "Yes, I truly
believe this!" There is no power in the belief in a
chronic condition. You have the power to rid yourself
of this belief and to claim your healing.

*Do you ever lose faith or feel that some conditions
are incurable?*

No, never! We receive too many good reports. I have

just been reading some of the letters that come to Silent Unity and they told of things that one could hardly believe, if he did not know God's power. These letters were from people who have been healed of all kinds of conditions.

For instance, one letter was from a mother whose son had been told that he had a growth on his lung and the doctor said it would have to be removed. The mother had asked for our prayers, and the son had great faith himself. He did not want to have the operation. Another examination only confirmed the doctor's judgment that the lung should be removed. But the son was not yet ready to give up on God's power to heal him. In the letter just received, the mother said that when the son went back to the doctor for further examination, the dark spot had entirely disappeared. The doctor said, "Well, this is a miracle!"

We have reports like this coming to Silent Unity every day. We never lose faith or feel discouraged, for we have seen people come through all kinds of problems, problems that to human appearance looked impossible.

We don't put any limit on God. Man may be limited but God is not—His power is unlimited.

Questions and Answers About Prayer

Tell us about prayer.

Prayer is the practice of the presence of God. Prayer is not just something we fall back on in some time of great need. In Unity we use affirmative prayer. Some persons ask how we can say, "This situation is not real," about a broken arm, for instance. We don't say it is not real, but we say it is a condition that needs to be changed. We recognize the spiritual nature. We are not just a body with a pain, but essentially a spiritual being.

Relaxation and prayer work are important. Silence, the inner realization of God's presence, has to be practiced. Keep practicing.

Eventually you will feel that you have touched the presence of God. The purpose of the silence is to contact the Spirit within you. God is present within you. God is omnipresent, but you contact His presence at the center of your being. Say to yourself, "Be still." Relax. Practice being quiet. Relax. Let go. Feel the presence.

When you say, "Our Father," in praying the Lord's Prayer, instead of thinking of God as being way out there somewhere, know that you are contacting the Lord of your own being within you.

Keep in mind that the Christ center is within and work from this center. In praying, remember that you are not praying to God outside you. God is everywhere, but you contact Him within.

We expect to eat three meals a day. Prayer is just as important. Spiritual ideas are spiritual food. Prayer consciousness is imperative till every thought is lined up with it. Some persons ask how long they should pray. It is not a matter of time; the consciousness of prayer is continual.

Remember that prayer is the practice of the presence of God. There is tremendous power in every prayer that acknowledges the presence and power of God. Your word is the working power of God. Christ is the living word in you, the power in you that speaks through your words of Truth with power and authority. Right now speak the word. Know that you are speaking the living word. Some persons wait to pray until they have some great need. Many others do not pray much, if at all. But prayer should become a habit, something that is constant. We can pray while driving a car, washing dishes, whatever we are doing, wherever we are. We develop a prayer consciousness, not just when there is a great need, but all the time as we practice living in the very presence of God.

How do you train yourself to pray more deeply?

Let prayer become a part of your life.
Put affirmative prayers into your mind.
Meet in mental agreement with Truth ideas.
Practice the presence of God.
Concentrate. Train the mind.
Repetition and agreement are both needed.

Jesus said that when we pray, we should ask in His name. Should we always pray in Jesus' name?

133

We believe in praying in the name of Jesus Christ. When people ask for healing prayers, we proclaim that they are healed, in the name of Jesus Christ. It doesn't make any difference what the condition is, because with God all things are possible.

A person has to arouse his own faith and cooperate with the idea of healing. He should take up a definite idea such as, *"God is my health, my wholeness, my harmony,"* or *"Divine order is established in my mind and body."* Then he should add this realization to his affirmation: *"In the name of Jesus Christ, I am healed."*

There is power and authority in the name of Jesus Christ. We think of Christ as representing the power of God and Jesus as the activity of that power. We invoke the power that Jesus stood for when we pray in His name. Jesus Christ represents power and authority in the realm of spiritual ideas. We are praying in the name of the greatest authority in the spiritual realm when we pray in the name of Jesus Christ.

It has been said that Charles Fillmore prayed from four to six hours a day. Is this true?

I would say that Charles Fillmore spent three-fourths of his time in prayer and meditation—night and day. This work really grew out of the inspiration and guidance he received in the silence. He constantly worked to prove the Truth in his own body and affairs, and he wanted others to share in the ideas that were revealed to him.

*If Charles Fillmore prayed three-fourths of his time,
it is amazing that he was able to do such a tremendous
work. Do you think that most of the ideas for his teachings and writing came to him during these times of
prayer and meditation?*

Yes, I am sure of it. I was in many classes conducted
by Mr. Fillmore. Sometimes as he answered the questions the students asked, it was as though he himself
was not answering the questions—it was the Holy Spirit
speaking through him. He lent himself wholeheartedly
to the Truth and opened his mind to the inspiration of
the Holy Spirit. This is something that more of us
should do. Jesus said, when His disciples asked Him
when He was going away, that the Father would send a
Comforter in His name. This Comforter is the Holy
Spirit, to which each of us has access. The Holy Spirit is
the movement or activity of the Christ within us.
Charles Fillmore felt the presence of the Holy Spirit. In
our Silent Unity healing work we always feel that there
is a power working in and through us. It is the Holy
Spirit, the activity of God in us, that does the work. We
never take personal credit for healing, nor did the
Fillmores.

Was Charles Fillmore truly inspired?

I asked Mr. Fillmore one time how he could write a
book like *Christian Healing* without revising or re-
writing it. He said: "Well, I will tell you, May. It all
came as a great inspiration. I wrote it down as it came."

I believe that he was truly inspired because he let the Holy Spirit move through him. I think that most of his books and articles were written in that way.

How many times should I repeat an affirmation of Truth?

The truth we decree reaches to the very depths of our being, to the subconscious level as well as to every other level. You have to stay with an affirmation long enough to change the pattern of your thinking and feeling. You have to absorb the idea of healing and have faith in the idea. Subconsciously, we may have been holding to a belief in sickness, we may have told ourselves that something is incurable, that we have had some condition for years. The words of Truth you speak are the word of God.

For example, "God is my health, I can't be sick" is an idea that can reach to the very depths of your being and purify, cleanse, and heal you. It is a matter of training; it is a matter of working with ideas so that they take root in your mind. It is more than repeating "God is my health, I can't be sick" and then in the next breath saying, "Oh, but my pain!" or "Everything is going badly." You see, you have to stay with the truth until you are convinced of it. You have to meet in agreement with the idea you are proclaiming. When you meet in agreement with ideas of life, strength, and wholeness, the subconscious phase of mind picks it up and puts it into action. But if you say one thing and believe another, you are at cross purposes.

136

What about affirmations and denials?

We say *yes* and *no* to everything in life, whether we realize it or not. We are choosing all the time—what we want and what we do not want. An affirmation is a way of saying *yes* to the Truth about ourself. *"I am a child of God, whole and perfect in every part"* is an affirmation. *"I do not believe in sickness, weakness, negation in any form"* is a denial. We deny what we do not want and affirm what we do want. The Unity prayer work is based on the affirmative-type prayer. We believe in affirming our oneness with God and with His power and perfection.

How can we be sure that we are praying effectively?

Real prayer takes practice. Speak the word, think the thought. Relax and let go and let God take over. Let God answer. Get the feeling of God's presence with you. This comes through the practice of prayer. You cannot get it out of a book.

If you have some particular need, you can say to God within you: "God, this is what I need. You take care of it." There is constructive power in thinking and speaking affirmative prayer. It is good also to take the words of Jesus. He said, "I am the light of the world" and He said, also, "You are the light of the world." Jesus' words are powerful. "I am the way, and the truth, and the life." Christ in you is showing you the way, He is the power within you. Jesus said, "Keep my sayings." You keep His sayings by affirming His words and taking them into your thoughts and heart.

137

Can you tell me in a few words what is unique about the Unity teachings?

Unity is a way of life, a way of prayer, a way of thinking and believing. It teaches one to accept the good. One of the things that I think is unique about the Unity teachings is what it teaches about the power of the word. Jesus said to keep His words. He said, "I am the way, and the truth, and the life." When we affirm the words of Jesus, this is one way in which we keep His words. We put them into our minds and we express them and use them. This is the idea behind affirmative prayer which we stress in Unity. An affirmation is based on Truth principles. We do not think of prayer as begging or beseeching God for something. Rather this kind of prayer is an acceptance of the good. We affirm: *"I am well, whole, strong. I am rich, prosperous, wise,"* and in doing so we are accepting the good and identifying ourself with it.

Should we pray an hour a day?

Prayer is not a matter of time, but of consciousness. Prayer is the practice of the presence of God. There is tremendous power in every prayer that acknowledges the presence and power of God. Mr. Fillmore practiced praying wherever he was. The word is the working power of the mind. Christ is the living Word. You are speaking the living word.

Some persons wait till they have a great need. Many persons do not pray much, or at all. But prayer isn't just sitting in a certain place for an hour or more. Prayer is a habit that we develop continually—while washing the dishes, driving a car, wherever we are, whatever we are doing. Through prayer we come to feel the presence and power of God. We develop a prayer consciousness, so that we are always aware of God's presence and power, not just when there is a great need, but all the time.

What is the most important thing to keep in mind when we pray?

When we say "Our Father" in praying the Lord's Prayer, instead of thinking of God as way out there somewhere, know that you are praying to the Lord of your own being. When you pray, "Forgive us our debts," know that the forgiving love of Christ is within you. His forgiving Spirit forgives every part of your nature. Keep in mind that there is the Christ center within you and work from this. Make contact in prayer with this spiritual center. Charles Fillmore said that the words, "Christ in you, the hope of glory" were the greatest words ever given to man.

The most important thing to remember in praying is that you are not praying to God outside yourself. God is everywhere, but you contact Him within. Christ is in the midst of you. Christ is the Word in you, the power in you that speaks through your words of Truth with power and authority.

As well as setting aside a special time each day for prayer, shouldn't we be in constant prayer, or at least in what would be called an attitude of prayer?

Yes, we should pray without ceasing. I think this means to keep our thoughts positive about things in life and not be negative, not dramatize everything we see or hear. Some people go to all the funerals, all the wrecks, talk about all the dire things that happen. They get some kind of satisfaction out of it. But I feel it is better to keep on the positive side.

Positive thinking is a way of praying without ceasing. We can feel surrounded by the presence of God, wherever we are, whatever we are doing. Like Brother Lawrence who practiced the Presence even as he worked among the pots and pans, we can practice the Presence as we go about the affairs of our daily life. We do not have to sit repeating affirmations; we can be living the Truth and knowing the Truth in the midst of activity.

This is literally what we do in Silent Unity: we pray without ceasing. You know, your every thought can be a prayer. Sometimes we don't realize it, but every positive thought is a kind of prayer, and we all have these good thoughts in our minds. We use them all the time. They constantly express through us. When we develop a Christ consciousness, that is the way we think all the time—on the positive side.

Is there a discipline to prayer?

Prayer isn't a hit-or-miss thing. Sometimes people pray just when they have some need. One of the wonderful things about the Silent Unity prayer ministry is that we pray every day, as regularly as the clock goes round. There is always someone in prayer, twenty-four hours a day, day and night. All of the workers come together in the morning at 8:00 for prayers; we have our healing service at 11:00 a.m. During the intervening hours each worker takes his turn at half-hour intervals, going into the Prayer Room to pray for all the names that have come in. Those who are answering the telephones in the Room of Light stop and pray many times during the hours they are there. We call this room the "Room of Light," for that is what it is. It is the room where a light is always shining, where someone is always praying.

There is tremendous power in prayer. For the most part, we haven't even tried it. As Alexis Carrel says, "Prayer is the greatest power known to man." But most of us don't use it. We need to practice prayer, to pray faithfully every day, year in and year out. This is what we do in Silent Unity. There is never a time when this prayer work isn't going on. I think the individual should form the habit of setting aside a certain time each day, a time when he says to himself, "This is my prayer time and I am going to be faithful to it." If we wait to pray until everything else is done—the time for prayer is always put off.

Do you specifically pray for something, or just assume that God knows what you are in need of? What if I want a new car, for instance?

When people ask for prayers for healing, we pray with them for healing. If they ask for financial help, we pray for their prosperity. As to praying for a new car, we would pray for your wisdom, guidance, and direction so that you would be led to the right car. And we would pray also that you would have an abundance to take care of your every need.

How do you know when you are getting guidance?

You feel it. Guidance does not always come as a direct answer. Many times it comes as a feeling of peace and rightness. And when guidance comes you find that you are taking some action, that you are doing something about the matter you have prayed for guidance on.

What are the techniques of prayer? Do you have to know special prayers? Some people say such beautiful prayers, others feel inadequate.

Unity prayers are practically all positive affirmations. We affirm the truth, such as: *"I am a child of God. I am whole, well, and free."* Or we may take a simple prayer such as the *The Prayer of Faith,* which has changed the lives of many persons. Many of these persons may remember only the first line of this prayer, "God is my help in every need." True prayer is not a matter of technique or beautiful words, but of an inner realization of our oneness with God and His good.

I would like to learn to meditate. How do I begin?

One way would be to begin with *Daily Word.* Take the prayer for the day and think about it, in other words, meditate upon it. Another way to begin your meditation is to read some verses in the Bible and think about their meaning, their bearing on your life.

To sit quietly and think about God, about Truth ideas, this is meditation. To open yourself to the inspiration of your indwelling Lord and then to listen for His inspiration, this is meditation.

How does one go into "the silence"?

Quietness comes first. Still the body. It takes practice to learn to be really still, just as it takes practice to become a musician. It may take years to learn to enter the silence. But we have to begin, we have to take time every day to be still. We may begin our time of silence by reading the Bible, or Unity books, or something that will help us to lift up our thinking. Then we meditate. The ideas that come to us in meditation will take hold in our consciousness.

The more we practice the silence, the more readily will we receive inspiration. In these times of quietness think of yourself as a spiritual being. Every part of you will respond, you will be lifted into a high place in consciousness. It is important to remember that the purpose of the silence is fulfilled as we practice the Truth that is revealed to us in our every day living. Right action should follow divine inspiration.

How do we know when we've really entered the silence?

The silence has to be practiced. Keep practicing. Eventually you will feel that you have touched the presence of God. The purpose of the silence is to contact the Spirit within you. God is present within you. God is omnipresent. But you contact His presence at the center of your being. Say to yourself, "Be still." Relax. Don't be fidgety. Practice being quiet. Let go. Feel God's presence and power within you and all about you.

The silence is not something mysterious. It is that inner place of stillness where you feel and know your oneness with God.

How do you build up your faith so that it is strong, firm, immovable?

Faith is strengthened as you speak your word. Every time your consciousness hears words of Truth you are building up your faith, you are strengthening your faith. This is why Charles Fillmore had the faith he had. He built it up by speaking the word. We encourage those who pray with us to speak words of Truth, not just once, but many times, every day. I think some persons say a prayer once and then put it aside, saying, "Oh, I did that and it didn't work." We have to be persistent and keep building in a consciousness of Truth.

The Art of Meditation

There are several facets to prayer. We should practice being quiet and taking time to meditate. By meditate I mean that we should take some simple idea to dwell on that brings us close to God in thought, then feel that God is going to speak to us in the silence of our own souls. Prayer is first important as a practice of the presence of God.

We should learn to practice the presence of God in every act of our life. We may ask, "How can I do this when I am busy all the time?" Brother Lawrence found God among the pots and pans. We can pray, or become conscious of the presence of God, even in the midst of everyday activity. Through practice we learn to feel the presence of God working in and through us at all times, no matter what we are doing.

Some persons spend much time and effort learning to play some musical instrument, or to play golf or some other sport, but they do not realize that time and effort are also required in learning how to meditate and pray. We need to learn to feel the all-enfolding presence of God always with us. And, I might add, not just when things are sunny, but when things seem more difficult to meet.

We can practice feeling the all-enfolding, loving presence of God in our quiet moments. Feel peace, feel poise, feel relaxation. Prayer is really based upon feeling. This feeling is a reaching out and then a reaching in for contact with the great, eternal Presence within and

145

without. This Presence must be felt around us wherever we are and within us. It takes practice to learn this. When we practice the art of meditation, we can enter into it at a moment's notice, wherever we are and whatever we are doing. We can learn never to let go the feeling of the Presence always with us. Through the practice of meditation and prayer, we can go through any experience easily and without losing undue energy.

Many times we pray with our problem uppermost in our mind, instead of releasing the problem to the intelligent Mind of Christ within us. If we release the problem, we will find many times that the answer is already ours.

One of the first steps in learning to pray is to practice the art of relaxation of mind and body. Say to yourself: "God in His great love created me. He is always with me. I trust Him. I relax and let go and feel His love within, around, and about me."

Say to any disturbed thought or feeling: "Peace, be still and know that I am God." Then say, "I relax and let go." Think of every part of your body as responding to this thought of relaxation. Relax from the top of your head to the soles of your feet. If you feel tension any place in your body say, "Relax and let go." The intelligence of God created your body, and it will respond to what you say.

Since God created your body as His temple, His presence is within you, waiting for you to give yourself to it freely without tension or anxiety. Say again to your thoughts, your emotions, your feelings, "Peace, be still." Then expect a great inner feeling of joy and peace to take over in your mind and body. Healing takes place the moment you surrender to the Lord of your being, which created you.

How much and how scientifically have you worked at developing the art of prayer? You will always get good answers to your prayers when you take the time to meditate and to pray. So make prayer an important part of your life. God bless you in your efforts.

Practice Feeling
the Presence of God

Through prayer and meditation we can transcend
our personal nature and touch the Spirit within us. An
early day metaphysical teacher used to have his students take this idea: "I transcend myself and all of my
affairs, for I am Spirit." There is great power in this idea
to lift us out of ourselves and our problems. We think of
ourselves most often from the physical or personal side
of our nature, overlooking the tremendous power of
our spiritual nature. This nature is awaiting our recognition and use.

When there seem to be problems in your life, or
when there are things piled up before you waiting your
attention, try laying hold of this idea in a very prayerful
way. Say to yourself: "I transcend myself and all of my
affairs, for I am Spirit." Everything in you quickly
responds to an idea like this. The intelligence of our
spiritual nature far transcends our everyday thinking.

"Do you not know that you are God's temple and
that God's Spirit dwells in you?" If we think of ourselves as a temple of God, we commence to see how
close we are to the source of our good.

We need quiet times of communion with God, times
when we are not asking for something, times when we
work consciously to cultivate the feeling of being in the
presence of God. Through the practice of meditation
we can establish a center of peace and quietness within.
We can turn to this center and gain great strength to
help us meet all of life's experiences. "All wisdom is in

silence given for every hourly need."

Since God created man out of the substance of His own being, your body is truly the temple of the living God. God did not create man and then separate Himself from His creation. As God's creation your body is truly His temple.

One Truth writer said: "Worship and adoration of God takes place in a church or temple and this means that our body should always be in a state of reverence for the Most High which has made it God's own dwelling place." This writer went on to say, "Often I call a little church service of my body cells and they sing together in reverent praise. The atoms of my body thrill to the good news that they are honored by the presence and the power of God within them."

Some of the scientists of this age are telling us that every atom in the body has a center of light. Think of the trillions of atoms in the body and think of the light that is radiating through them. Your body is truly a temple of light. Dr. Donald Hatch Andrews, who was for years professor of chemistry at John Hopkins University, states in his book *The Symphony of Life:* "Actually at this moment you are filled with a kind of symbolic light. And not only are you filled with it, you are radiating it, and this can be proved in the laboratory."

This is in accord with Jesus' teaching. We see that He literally meant what He said when He proclaimed: "I am the light of the world," and "You are the light of the world."

Think of this wonderful body temple as filled with light and you will let go the old materialistic idea that the body is heavy, mass, and material. You will never again think of your body in that way. Instead of looking at just the surface appearance of your body, look within to the radiant, beautiful self of you, living in the temple of God.

In order to establish the body in a feeling of light and harmony, it is good to practice recognizing the light and harmony in the body. This can follow the form of a little drill in the silence.

First, let us think of the body as a temple in which the light is shining in every part. All the atoms of light in your body will respond and rejoice because you are recognizing their worth and beauty.

Remember that your body is a very intelligent instrument of God. You can send your thought into every part of your body and it will rejoice and respond to your thought and your word.

You can still any disturbing thoughts by saying in the quietness within you, "Be still, and know that I am God." Then practice being still in conformity with your word. Usually one's mind is so filled with thoughts about the outer life and affairs that it takes time to learn to be still. Say to your mind and your thoughts, "Be still, and know that I am God." Feel quietness, feel peace. To those troubled emotions that usually center around the heart, say, "Be still, and know that I am peace." This is a recognition of God in the temple as a center of radiating peace. You can also say to the heart center, "Be still, and know that I am love." Then feel God's love flowing in and through every area of your being—mind, body, and emotions—healing every hurt.

151

If you should feel that conditions or circumstances are overpowering you, center your attention in your throat and say, "All power is given unto me in mind and in body." That within you which says "All power is given unto me" is the voice of the Christ within you, proclaiming spiritual power and mastery over conditions of mind, body, and affairs.

Relax through your shoulders and the back of your neck and say, "I relax and let go all tension, stress, and strain." As you say this, follow through by relaxing and feeling relaxed.

Next think of your back and say, "I am strong in the Lord and in the power of His might." Almost immediately you will feel a surge of strength. One of our Unity teachers was healed of tuberculosis by taking these words from the Bible and affirming them, "Let the weak say, I am strong."

You can follow this formula of blessing every part of your body temple. To do so prayerfully and regularly is to recognize the light, life, and intelligence within you. As you use these words, "Be still, and know that I am life," think of the life that is flowing throughout your body. Your arms and hands will tingle with life in a short time. You can use this same idea, "Be still, and know that I am life," and feel this life in and through every part of your body, down to the soles of your feet.

Directing your attention to every part of the body and speaking words of life, brings a feeling of healing, renewing, restoring life wherever it is needed. This is a wonderful healing treatment.

"In him was life, and the life was the light of men. The light shines in the darkness, and the darkness has not overcome it."

When you have taken time to relax and to feel that God is moving in and through every part of your mind and body, you will feel restored and renewed. You will feel the light and life of Christ radiant within you.

Serenity through Prayer

When I was in the South recently one of our good, faithful friends who has been a Truth student for years told me how much benefit she had received through Unity methods of prayer.

This friend said: "I wish Unity would emphasize the need for more prayer, meditation, and the silence. Unity should teach people to do their own overcoming through prayer."

We do certainly try to emphasize the necessity of daily prayer, which is our method of communion with God. Perhaps the most important teaching of Unity is the necessity for meditation and prayer. We teach the art of learning to be quiet. We need, as Paul says, to study to be quiet. It takes practice and study to learn to quiet our thoughts and emotions.

We need to take time to listen to the inspiration that will come to us through prayer and meditation.

It is not praying hard or vigorously that brings results. Ease of prayer comes through our steady devotion to it.

Emerson said some wonderful things about prayer: "Prayer is the sincere effort to know God," and, "Prayer is the contemplation of the facts of life from the highest point of view."

Serenity is attained through putting God first in everything, every day of our life. By turning our attention to God regularly and under all circumstances and conditions we become assured that all is right with our world, that God is in charge. Daily prayer becomes an effortless way. We form the habit of prayer, and eventually we learn the art of praying without ceasing, without effort or strain.

Prayer is the most accumulative and productive power in the world. It draws out of our inner self the ideas and strength we need. Through prayer we keep in touch with a constant flow of divine ideas always ready to sustain us in any emergency.

God is. I am. We are one, and I am His perfect expression. These things we learn through daily prayer.

The wisdom we need, the power we need, the courage we need, the love we need, the peace we need we can always draw out of the reservoir of spiritual power within us. We can draw on this unlimited power at a moment's notice.

The place of prayer is sometimes called the "secret place of the Most High," or the "kingdom of God within." By whatever name we call it, it is always there for our use.

David Sarnoff has said: "Man has not yet learned to keep step with science. He has become technologically mature, but is spiritually adolescent. Now that he has learned to conquer nature, he must learn to conquer himself."

In the realm of Spirit lies the challenge of the future. We are living in an age of change and movement. It is an age of automation and communication.

Dr. John Harvey Furbay, Director of Cultural and Education Services for Trans World Airlines, has made some remarkable comments in relation to what he has discovered in his travels on four continents. In one of his eye-opening lectures on the subject of this changing world he says that change has reached every part of the world, all the faraway places. He says that the great unrest in the world today is perhaps because backward nations are commencing to realize how the rest of the world lives and they want to be a part of it. They do not find conditions in their country the same as ours and the rest of the world. They want equal opportunities.

For centuries there were people who had no communication with the rest of the world. During the past few years radio and television have become a part of the lives of all the peoples of the world. What we do and what we communicate by radio and television can reach every country of the world in a matter of minutes. The time of isolation of any group is past. Nothing can be hidden as the Bible states: "Nothing is covered that will not be revealed, or hidden that will not be known."

It takes patience, growth, and development, as well as great understanding to keep up with what is happening in the world.

We are not only living in a new age but we have to adjust to the times. There are some who still long for the good old days. But these good old days will never return. Some persons do not wish to live in changing times. However, it is only a small per cent of the people of the world who would rather live in their thoughts and dreams of the past. Most people are alive to the growing and developing world and the progress of the peoples of the world.

No one can hold back. We need to keep facing the light and moving forward. Some persons think the world is static and fixed. But when one stops to think he realizes that this world is constantly moving, whirling around the sun every day. We are moving whether we want to or not.

There is something very important for all of us to learn in this fast moving world. It is essential that we discover our own spiritual center and live our life from this center. In other words, we can keep our balance in this great and beautiful world of ours if we do not live on the outer fringe of change and excitement and learn to live at the center of our being, through meditation and prayer.

Sometimes people become emotionally and physically disturbed because they do not know how to handle their reaction to all that goes on in the world. We, in Unity, learn to be quiet. Quiet does not always come easily to people. But through daily practice we learn its value. "In quietness and in trust shall be your strength."

Unity teaches that all power has its birth in silence. All reforms must begin with their cause which is in mind, as mind does all its real work in the realm of silence.

I remember visiting a World's Fair in which a special building was erected to house a tremendous power wheel. The building was called the Machinery Building, and there were two things which interested me in this building.

There was the tremendous wheel that was moving so fast that you could not see it move at its center. And not a sound could be heard. It was a great giant of power and produced tremendous energy.

Not too far away there was a little machine that was fastened to the floor, a machine not much larger than the old-fashioned sewing machine. It chugged and groaned and made a terrific rattling noise. It was not producing much but noise.

The really great man who accomplishes things generates the power within him in quietness. The little fellow who sputters and fusses and makes a lot of noise and never gets quiet is not very effective.

All great men who express great ideas take time to think, to meditate, and to pray.

The tendency of our times is to get people to act, go, do, buy, take. All selling campaigns are promoted through action verbs. Before we know it, if we are not thinking, we are hypnotized by these words.

Someway we have grown to feel that the mind should be used every moment, that we should be thinking, affirming, planning, talking, or the mind will grow stale.

We do not hop, skip, and jump, and exercise the physical body all the time, though we believe in exercise. Neither should we be pushing ourselves mentally or planning everything for ourselves and others.

Rest the mind for a while by feeling just the joy of living.

Many persons never feel at peace because they do not know this simple truth: God did not leave you, but is always within you. This quotation from the writings of Charles Fillmore makes it very clear the way God has provided for us: "Many have caught sight of the fact that the true church of Christ is a state of consciousness in man, but few have gone so far in the realization as to

159

know that in the very body of each man and woman is a temple in which the Christ holds religious services at all times."

As a man's faith is aroused through prayer he builds a background in his life from which to meet emergencies. He finds the strength and the courage to meet whatever comes to him.

Through prayer we arouse our own spiritual nature and activate God's power within us. We find the beginning of the solution to our problems by accepting Jesus' invitation, "Come to me, all who labor and are heavy laden, and I will give you rest."

We find serenity through prayer; we find power and peace in the silence.

Helps along the Way

There is a spiritual power within us so tremendous that when we put it into action it transforms our life.

God has not left us alone to work out our own salvation. When God created us, He placed His kingdom within us. The kingdom of God is a spiritual center in the midst of each one of us. Remember when Jesus was asked where the kingdom was, He answered, "The kingdom of God is in the midst of you." Since the kingdom of God is in the midst of us, then surely we must be very close to Him. Let us awaken to this truth and commence to let God's Spirit find expression through us. It is up to us to rise up and use the power which is our birthright as children of God. Those who do this find life rich, expanding, and joyous.

We have looked too long at the appearances which make up the "come and go" of our everyday living which constantly changes. One day we call an appearance good, the next day we may call it bad or wrong. We have judged ourself and others from a limited standard.

Also, we have not recognized the body as the temple of the living God. Perhaps the greatest difficulties which our body experiences are caused by our emotional upsets.

As we commence to realize that we are spiritual beings, life takes on a new aspect. Through this recognition of our spiritual nature we touch the power which controls all of life. We learn how to handle our mental, emotional, and spiritual needs. From the standpoint of the Christ in us, our God Self, we have control of our life's experiences. Through this spiritual control, our body and our life cease to be battlegrounds for uncontrolled emotions and feelings.

Through the Mind of Christ in us we discover our spiritual nature. "Christ in you, the hope of glory" is Paul's great teaching.

How do we discover and learn to lay hold of the power within us? First by being open and receptive to the idea that there is such a power for us to use. Then we seek this power through meditation and prayer, so that we can touch it within our hearts or our feeling nature.

We can speak to God in this way: "God, reveal Yourself to me so that I can understand and feel Your presence always with me." We should take some time every day to be quiet, to practice the presence of God. As we do this we will have a feeling of great peace, we will feel surrounded by light, the light of God's presence, we will feel His love enfolding us. We will feel God's presence blessing our mind, our heart, our body, and expanding through our thoughts and feelings until it includes all of our life's experiences. As we come into the awareness of God's presence and learn to abide there, we find that we bless others. We find that there is no limit to the good that can be accomplished through our expanding consciousness.

The following adaptation of the meditation "A Transcendent Treatment" has been a part of my personal notebook for many years. The original meditation was written by Rexford B. Jeffery, who was one of the first metaphysical teachers of Charles and Myrtle Fillmore. The following affirmations are a wonderful spiritual treatment for yourself or for others. Any line is powerful. In Silent Unity we frequently affirm, "I transcend myself and all of my affairs, for I am Spirit." Try meditating on these transcendent ideas and see what a lift you will feel.

As Moses lifted up the serpent in the wilderness, even so must I be lifted up.

In my integrity within me, where I know and see as God, I know and see myself, to be free, wise, immortal.

I am unfettered and unbound, triumphant, glorious, splendid.

I am unweighted by human thought of limitation, unweighted by matter.

I am unbound, undiseased, buoyant.

I am strong, mighty, forceful, powerful, divine.

My eye is lit by fire from on high.

My tongue is tipped with celestial instructions.

I am bright, joyous.

I am victorious, undaunted.

I am spotless, beautiful.

I am deathless, abiding.

I am flawless, fearless, transcending myself and all of my affairs, independent.

I am smiling, sound, sane, strong.

I am the strong Son of God, brother of Jesus Christ and joint heir of the Father to the kingdom.

I am alive with God and upheld by His free Spirit forever.

All the world sees me as I see myself, now and evermore.

Use the Working Power
of the Holy Spirit

There is a tremendous, unused power available at all times. It is ready to be called into action! This is the power of the Holy Spirit. But it doesn't come into expression in you until you call upon it! Anyone who has felt the baptism of the Holy Spirit will tell you that it is a beautiful and wonderful experience.

We think of the Trinity as consisting, first of the loving Father, God; then His Son, Jesus Christ; the third member of the Trinity is the Holy Spirit, which puts the ideas of the Father and the Son into expression in our lives. It is not at all complex to think of the Trinity in this way—God, the Father, Jesus Christ, the Son, and the Holy Spirit, the activity of spiritual power.

Jesus knew that we needed a personal helper, and this is what the Holy Spirit is—a very personal and present help. You may remember that Jesus said many things about the Holy Spirit. In the 14th Chapter of John we read: "I will pray the Father, and he will give you another Counselor, to be with you for ever, even the Spirit of truth."

Jesus tells us the blessings to be gained through the recognition of the Holy Spirit. "These things I have spoken to you, while I am still with you. But the Counselor, the Holy Spirit, whom the Father will send in my name, he will teach you all things, and bring to your remembrance all that I have said to you." Jesus referred often to the Holy Spirit and the Spirit of truth. Re-

165

member these words? "When the Spirit of truth comes, he will guide you into all the truth."

Thus you are assured that you have an inner guide, willing to direct you, to speak through you. Be open and receptive in your mind and listen to this wonderful Helper.

When you let the Holy Spirit come into your consciousness it will carry out God's perfect plan for your life. It puts all of your good thoughts and words and prayers into action with power and authority.

When you pray that God's will be done in you and when a strong conviction comes to you as to what you shall do, then let the Holy Spirit act through you to bring your good into expression.

When anyone is willing to dedicate himself to cooperate with God in doing His work he becomes a channel through which the Holy Spirit moves to bless, to heal, and to restore.

The Holy Spirit sheds its light and love through any group of people who have love for humanity and want to pour out a blessing upon people everywhere. Vibrations of a high order are released through contacting the light of the Holy Spirit and these vibrations bring about healing. I believe that this is the power behind the Unity work, and especially the healing work of Silent Unity.

The Holy Spirit is very important to anyone who is in need of healing. We all need to be filled and refilled with an outpouring of the Holy Spirit. As we open ourselves to the Holy Spirit, we will be renewed, healed, and restored in mind, body, and soul.

The Holy Spirit will take over at any moment it is

invited to speak through you, to lead you, to heal you, and to fill your heart with love, compassion, and understanding. Since the Holy Spirit represents God in action, we need to use this power to act through us, to heal us, to speak through us.

When we have prayed and asked the Holy Spirit to take over, it will flood our whole being, not so much with excessive emotional feeling, but as a warm, loving presence that literally speaks and acts through us and for us.

Try calling upon the Holy Spirit to move through you and to act through you. Many times when I have been very busy and seemed not to be making much headway, I have simply said, "Holy Spirit, take over." Try this sometime and see how wonderfully the Holy Spirit responds.

It is good to feel that the Holy Spirit speaks through us, infills us, warms us, and releases us from anxieties. When I have taught classes, I have asked that the Holy Spirit will take over and pour out its blessing upon me and all of us.

If it is necessary for you to get up before the public and address a group, talk to the Holy Spirit in this way: "Holy Spirit, express Your ideas through me in perfect thoughts and words."

All that the Holy Spirit needs is the invitation and when you call upon it the ideas, the wisdom, and the words come flowing through into expression.

In Charles Fillmore's writings he states, "The word of Truth in me is not idle, but it is quietly spreading from point to point and the process will continue until my whole consciousness is vitalized by the Holy

Spirit."

The Holy Spirit has come to people of faith throughout the ages. It has acted through them to illumine them, to inspire them, to protect them, to heal them, and best of all to shine through them. When we call upon it, the Holy Spirit will flood us with its power. It will come to us as a presence of love, light, beauty, and understanding, and it will bring to our remembrance all the beautiful teachings of Jesus Christ.

Listen to these words of Jesus and try to apply them: "Do not be anxious beforehand what you are to say; but say whatever is given you in that hour, for it is not you who speak, but the Holy Spirit."

Stay tuned in to the wisdom, direction, and guidance of this tremendous power within you. The Spirit of truth will release its inspired ideas through you and they will flow freely through you.

Speaking of the Holy Spirit, Jesus said, "He will glorify me, for he will take what is mine and declare it to you." What a tremendous representation of the Holy Spirit was Jesus Christ!

Following are some ideas for prayers that you may use in developing your consciousness along these lines:

For Healing:

The loving, powerful action of the Holy Spirit takes command in my body, and I am renewed and restored.

For Rejuvenation:

The rejuvenating power of the Holy Spirit is now at work in every atom and function of my body, making me alive and radiant with life and wholeness.

For Your Longing Soul:

The inspiration of the Holy Spirit reaches to the depths of my soul and satisfies my every need.

When You Have a Problem to Solve:

Dear loving Spirit within me, I give this problem over to you. I relax and let You direct its outworking.

When in Need of Comfort:

The comforting, sustaining presence of the Holy Spirit uplifts and strengthens me.

For Help in Your Work:

The Holy Spirit, expressing itself through me, touches all that concerns me and brings order and harmony into my work (or life).

For Prosperity:

I let the Holy Spirit take command of my affairs and I am prospered through new avenues of supply.

Finding the True God

In ways innumerable we have been seeking for God through the ages. We have sought Him in this church and in that church, expecting Him to be revealed to us in some mysterious way by the minister. But Jesus Christ said to us, "Nor will they say, 'Lo, here it is!' or 'There!' for behold, the kingdom of God is in the midst of you." And so we must seek Him within ourself.

We can seek God as wisdom, as supreme power, as undeviating law, as never-failing principle, but first let us recognize Him as a God of love enthroned in our own heart. We shall then know that there is nothing to fear in His law. His love is just and forgiving. There is nothing to fear in His absolute power, for He is also absolute love. He is the changeless principle of love that is always good. He is not a God of impulses who sometimes wills good and sometimes wills evil for His children.

Can you think of a God of love as one who would will sickness, poverty, and even death upon His children in the face of this teaching: "For God so loved the world that he gave his only Son, that whoever believes in him should not perish but have eternal life"?

Let us not abide in hard man-made conditions, imagining that God so wills it. Let us rise out of this error belief. Never does the God of love will for us anything but what He is Himself: absolute perfection, perfection not only in our spiritual nature but perfection expressed in our body and radiated in our affairs.

When the love of God takes possession of your heart,

171

all resentment, all enmity, all thoughts of injustice disappear. You find the love of God shining into the dark corners, cleansing, brightening, and purifying all that is unlike Him. His love wipes out the mistakes of the past and gives a new day filled with innumerable blessings.

Love is the supreme gift to man, and you cannot mistake its Christlike quality when it comes into your consciousness. It gives instead of taking for itself. It looses those who have been held in personal bondage. It frees; it forgives; it heals.

When you touch the love of God in your heart, you find yourselves wanting to do something to bless and help others, even as Jesus Christ blessed and helped. The more you give out of this wonderful gift which is yours, the more comes back to you of heavenly blessings. You find peace, happiness, health, harmony, and prosperity, for you have found the real source of that which satisfies.

God the Source

When Storms Come

In each of us is a quality that is called faith. Perhaps we have never considered how much our lives depend upon our faith.

When faith is rightfully placed—that is, when it is fixed upon that which is true and uplifting—it makes us strong, masterful, and courageous. The individual who believes in the good, in spite of appearances to the contrary, becomes so poised and so secure in his mind that when the winds blow and the waves come he stands unmoved, for he is like the man to whom Jesus referred when he said:

"Every one . . . will be like a wise man who built his house upon the rock: and the rain fell, and the floods came, and the winds blew and beat upon that house, but it did not fall, because it had been founded on the rock."

We are establishing our faith upon a rock when we give the substance of our thinking to that which is true, holy, pure. We are establishing our faith on a firm foundation when we believe in the goodness, the uprightness, and the honesty of our fellow man. But, above all, let us always hold fast to the love and the goodness of God. Doing that, we can always stand unmoved during the storm; we can meet the test, because our strength and our endurance are from God. The one who trusts in God is always protected. He abides in peace with the full assurance that all is well.

I Am the Christ within You

A Meditation

I have been with you from the beginning of time. I shall continue to be with you throughout eternity. If you will but tune your ear to listen to Me, I will guide you safely through every experience of life.

No matter how many times you may have stumbled along the way, I have forgiven you and put you back on your feet.

I surround you with My love so that you may have a feeling of security.

I am the loving Christ Spirit within you. Let Me heal your mind and your body. Let Me heal your heart when something troubles you. Turn your anxieties and your fears over to Me. I will give you peace.

I will harmonize and adjust all your reactions to life's experiences. You need not worry or fret. Go happily on your way. Accept Me as the constant, loving Presence with you, and I will not fail you. Learn of Me. Trust Me.

Affirmations
from My Personal Notebook

"This I believe . . ."
Begin your prayer-affirmations with this statement. It will strengthen your faith.

"Thank You, Father . . ."
The power of praise can bring about seeming miracles. End all your prayer times with a word of thanksgiving.

For Youth and Beauty:

My life processes are perpetuating the youth ideas in my body. Every atom, every cell is renewed. Old ideas, any idea of age is eliminated from my mind and erased from my body. My life processes are stamped by the renewing, youth-giving idea, and I am eternally young. & healthy

I eat only the food required for a healthy, youthful body. My perfect weight is ____ pounds, and I give thanks for that perfect weight. I am youthful, graceful, healthy.

My appetite is under the control and direction of Spirit; therefore I do not overeat. My appetites are satisfied through Spirit.

I am the ever-renewing, the ever-unfolding expression of infinite life and youth. My eyes, my ears, and all my faculties are quickened and renewed through the

177

youthful life processes working in and through my being.

I *am* yo*ung*, str*ong*, *healthy*. My body knows it. My body shows it.

I am young, because I am perpetually *being renewed*; my life comes new every moment from the infinite source of life. I am new every morning and fresh every evening because I *live*, *move*, and have my being in Him who is *the source of* all *life*. I am constantly renewed, constantly refreshed.

Through Christ in me, my brain cells are rejuvenated. My mind is keen, alert, and intelligent.

I am young, always young, strong, buoyant. I cannot grow old and decrepit, because in the truth of my being, I am divine, and divine principle cannot age. My mind constantly creates the youth pattern instead of the pattern of age.

God-life has perfect expression in my circulation—through my veins and arteries.

I am always fresh and youthful, rested and relaxed. I feel *young*, act *young*, and look young, for truly I am Spirit. and Sp cannot age or be impaired

For Healing

I send my healing word to the depths of my being,

178

and every atom of my body accepts it and responds. I am cleansed, purified, and made new. The atoms of my body shout for joy. This I decree in the name of Jesus Christ.

For Divine Love

My heart is filled with love. I am not critical, irritable, or impatient. I am the love of God in expression.

To Develop Your Potential

I see myself as God sees me, glorious, splendid, beloved, strong, well, and capable. I see the world as a beautiful place in which to grow and work and play. Through the power of the Christ within me I revive my ability to live happily, to give good service generously, and to inspire those who, like me, are growing and working and playing.

To Realize One's Worth

I am the radiant, all-wise, all-loving, all-conquering son of God. I rule supreme in all the affairs of mind and body. Infinite wisdom guides me, divine love prospers me, and I am successful in all that I undertake. I am the ever-renewing, ever-unfolding expression of infinite life, love, and wisdom.

To Overcome Fear

I place myself lovingly in the hands of God. He

protects me. He watches over me. There is nothing to fear.

For Peace

Almighty Father, let there be peace on earth and let it begin with love and peace in my heart. I accept peace from within myself, from God. I open the way for greater peace by letting go of all tendencies to hate, to condemn, to find fault, to become disturbed and use unkind, bitter words. I remember the Christ and the Christ Way, forgetting all else. Lord, make me an instrument of Thy peace.

For Giving a Talk

I believe in God as the source of all inspiration.

He is the never-failing fountain of all ideas.

I am God's child endowed with His intelligence and wisdom.

I express my thoughts in a clear, logical, convincing manner.

My voice takes on a new sweetness and depth.

My voice is rich and warm, strong, and vibrant.

I speak so as to give my listeners an instant, clear, logical, pleasant and interesting insight into any subject under discussion.

I speak in a clear, pleasing, and interesting way.

I create and maintain a clear, convincing style.

I present each subject in a vital, wholesome, fresh way.

I have a dependable, retentive, and photographic memory.

I maintain a clear, definite contact with Divine Mind.

I sustain a constant flow of rich and interesting ideas.

181

I sustain a constant flow of fresh, unusual ideas on any subject desired.

I contact God's power instantly, easily, and naturally, and I apply it to my work successfully.

I realize this contact with universal mind constantly and without interruption.

Through my contact with universal mind I have flowing into my mind and out again to the world, ideas that are divine, inspired, rich, productive, wholesome, charming, and convincing.

With ease I put these ideas into clear, definite forms.

I constantly speak ideas that are rich, inspired, productive, wholesome, charming, and convincing.

Printed U.S.A.

116-F-8541-5M-7-86

8

26
29
-30
36

65

N 69

N 73

109

114 - aging

Sp intelligence
165 "   (171) Sp chapter
171
173

138 prayer is
140   "
142 How u know

145
149
150
153
161
163